Understanding World History

The Early Middle Ages

Adam Woog

Bruno Leone
Series Consultant

ReferencePoint Press®

San Diego, CA

My thanks go to Stu Witmer for generously sharing his knowledge.

© 2012 ReferencePoint Press, Inc.
Printed in the United States

For more information, contact:
ReferencePoint Press, Inc.
PO Box 27779
San Diego, CA 92198
www.ReferencePointPress.com

LIBRARY OF CONGRESS CATALOGING-IN-PUBLICATION DATA

Woog, Adam, 1953-
The early Middle Ages / by Adam Woog.
  p. cm. — (Understanding world history series)
Includes bibliographical references and index.
ISBN-13: 978-1-60152-151-4 (hardcover)
ISBN-10: 1-60152-151-0 (hardcover)
 1. Middle Ages—Juvenile literature. 2. Civilization, Medieval—Juvenile literature. 3. Europe—History—476–1492—Juvenile literature. 4. Feudalism—Europe—History—Juvenile literature. 5. Europe—Church history—600–1500—Juvenile literature. I. Title.
 D117.W66 2011
 940.1'2--dc22
                                                          2010039210

Contents

Foreword

When the Puritans first emigrated from England to America in 1630, they believed that their journey was blessed by a covenant between themselves and God. By the terms of that covenant they agreed to establish a community in the New World dedicated to what they believed was the true Christian faith. God, in turn, would reward their fidelity by making certain that they and their descendants would always experience his protection and enjoy material prosperity. Moreover, the Lord guaranteed that their land would be seen as a shining beacon—or in their words, a "city upon a hill,"—which the rest of the world would view with admiration and respect. By embracing this notion that God could and would shower his favor and special blessings upon them, the Puritans were adopting the providential philosophy of history—meaning that history is the unfolding of a plan established or guided by a higher intelligence.

The concept of intercession by a divine power is only one of many explanations of the driving forces of world history. Historians and philosophers alike have subscribed to numerous other ideas. For example, the ancient Greeks and Romans argued that history is cyclical. Nations and civilizations, according to these ancients of the Western world, rise and fall in unpredictable cycles; the only certainty is that these cycles will persist throughout an endless future. The German historian Oswald Spengler (1880–1936) echoed the ancients to some degree in his controversial study *The Decline of the West.* Spengler asserted that all civilizations inevitably pass through stages comparable to the life span of a person: childhood, youth, adulthood, old age, and, eventually, death. As the title of his work implies, Western civilization is currently entering its final stage.

Joining those who see purpose and direction in history are thinkers who completely reject the idea of meaning or certainty. Rather, they reason that since there are far too many random and unseen factors at work on the earth, historians would be unwise to endorse historical predictability of any type. Warfare (both nuclear and conventional), plagues, earthquakes, tsunamis, meteor showers, and other catastrophic world-changing events have loomed large throughout history and prehistory. In his essay "A Free Man's Worship," philosopher and mathematician Bertrand Russell (1872–1970) supported this argument, which many refer to as the nihilist or chaos theory of history. According to Russell, history follows no preordained path. Rather, the earth itself and all life on earth resulted from, as Russell describes it, an "accidental collocation of atoms." Based on this premise, he pessimistically concluded that all human achievement will eventually be "buried beneath the debris of a universe in ruins."

Whether history does or does not have an underlying purpose, historians, journalists, and countless others have nonetheless left behind a record of human activity tracing back nearly 6,000 years. From the dawn of the great ancient Near Eastern civilizations of Mesopotamia and Egypt to the modern economic and military behemoths China and the United States, humanity's deeds and misdeeds have been and continue to be monitored and recorded. The distinguished British scholar Arnold Toynbee (1889–1975), in his widely acclaimed 12-volume work entitled *A Study of History,* studied 21 different civilizations that have passed through history's pages. He noted with certainty that others would follow.

In the final analysis, the academic and journalistic worlds mostly regard history as a record and explanation of past events. From a more practical perspective, history represents a sequence of building blocks—cultural, technological, military, and political—ready to be utilized and enhanced or maligned and perverted by the present. What that means is that all societies—whether advanced civilizations or preliterate tribal cultures—leave a legacy for succeeding generations to either embrace or disregard.

Recognizing the richness and fullness of history, the ReferencePoint Press Understanding World History series fosters an evaluation and interpretation of history and its influence on later generations. Each volume in the series approaches its subject chronologically and topically, with specific focus on nations, periods, or pivotal events. Primary and secondary source quotations are included, along with complete source notes and suggestions for further research.

Moreover, the series reflects the truism that the key to understanding the present frequently lies in the past. With that in mind, each series title concludes with a legacy chapter that highlights the bonds between past and present and, more important, demonstrates that world history is a continuum of peoples and ideas, sometimes hidden but there nonetheless, waiting to be discovered by those who choose to look.

Important Events in the Early Middle Ages

ca. 400
Beginning around this time and for the next 400 years, barbarian tribes rule the segmented lands that formerly made up the Roman Empire.

456
The Western Roman Empire falls and is replaced by many small, fragmented kingdoms; many historians mark this as the beginning of the early Middle Ages.

285
The Roman Empire splits into western and eastern halves.

715
The Muslim conquest reaches its height, extending from the Pyrenees Mountains in southern France to China.

300   400   500   600   700

ca. 482
Clovis, founder of the Merovingian dynasty, becomes king of the Franks, the beginning of a golden age for that part of Europe.

751
The Carolingian dynasty succeeds the Merovingian.

570
Muhammad, the founder of Islam, is born in Arabia.

380
Christianity becomes the official religion of the Roman Empire, foreshadowing the later conversion of all of Europe.

ca. 565
Beginning around this time and continuing for the next few decades, the Eastern Roman Empire loses much of its land to invaders, and Byzantine power begins to weaken.

771
Charlemagne becomes king of the Franks and brings that realm to its height of power and influence.

ca. 889
The first city commune, an organization of citizens banded together for protection and mutual aid, is formed in the Italian town of Forlì.

962
Otto the Great is crowned emperor by Pope John XII, marking the beginning of the Holy Roman Empire.

1000s
The first universities are founded, in the Islamic world and in Bologna, Italy, and Paris, France.

800
Charlemagne is crowned Roman emperor by Pope Leo III, marking an important point in the ongoing alliance between church and state.

800   **850**   **900**   **950**   **1000**

888
The decline of the Frankish Empire, the first unified kingdom in Europe since the Roman Empire, begins.

1096
The First Crusade, a religious war in which European Christians sought to reclaim the Holy Land from Islamic forces, begins; many historians mark this date as the end of the early Middle Ages.

814
Charlemagne dies, bringing to an end the peak of medieval Frankish civilization.

ca. 771
The Frankish Empire expands, covering much of the European continent, and presides over the blossoming of knowledge and reforms called the Carolingian Renaissance.

The Defining Characteristics of the Early Middle Ages

For nearly a thousand years, Rome dominated much of the European continent. After the Roman Empire split into eastern and western halves in AD 285, this sprawling realm began to weaken. The Eastern Roman Empire survived—and mostly thrived—for centuries; the Western Roman Empire dissolved in AD 456. To many historians the end of the Western Roman Empire marks the beginning of the Middle Ages. At this point, one of the most important periods in European history made way for another. This new era was radically different, but like its predecessor, it was crucial to the evolution of Western civilization.

Were the Dark Ages Really Dark?

The Middle Ages (or medieval era), broadly speaking, were the thousand years between the middle of the 400s and the beginning of the next period—the Renaissance—in the mid-1400s. Historians often view the Middle Ages in two periods: The early Middle Ages, from about 456 to 1000, and the late Middle Ages, from about 1000 to 1450. While civilizations in China, India, and the Middle East were reaching new heights in government, technology, the arts, mathematics, and other areas during the Middle Ages, in many ways the early Middle Ages was a dismal period in European history—one of poverty, repression, violence, and ignorance. Education was rare. Few people could read. A strict religion controlled daily life. Medicine was crude and helpless against the frequent plagues and other ills that befell the population. Wars were frequent. And a rigid social system ensured that social classes were kept apart.

Long ago, this bleak picture gave rise to a popular nickname for the early Middle Ages: the Dark Ages. The Dark Ages was often seen as an unproductive period between more enlightened times: the Roman Empire and the late Middle Ages. In some ways this portrait is accurate, but it is incomplete. Much of what is known today about the Middle Ages comes from written documents that have survived the ravages of time. But some of what modern historians believe about the early Middle Ages may not be provable, due to exaggerations, falsehoods, and legends passed down through the centuries. Nonetheless, beneath its seemingly dreary surface, the early Middle Ages saw dramatic shifts—and, often, improvements—in Europe's government, religion, and society.

Charlemagne

Among the shifts were fundamental changes in the structure of politics and government. These were at first brought about as the Roman Empire collapsed. Western Europe fragmented, and what had once been a unified dominion devolved into a loose patchwork of tribes and kingdoms, each with its own leaders and concerns.

Some of these rulers tried to unify the various groups into a single, centralized government that could operate in the spirit of the former empire. The one who came closest was the most influential figure of the era: Charlemagne, the king of the Franks in the late 700s and early 800s. Charlemagne ambitiously expanded his empire until, at its peak in the 800s, it covered a significant part of the continent. The dominion he controlled would in time form the framework for the map of modern-day Europe.

Charlemagne was also the driving force behind important reforms in economics, social structure, the arts, and education. The

Roman Empire had always placed a high value on education and the spirit of inquiry, and Charlemagne's reforms were a deliberate return to these values. Pierre Riché, a distinguished historian of the Middle Ages, comments that Charlemagne "enjoyed an exceptional destiny, and by the length of his reign, by his conquests, legislation and legendary stature, he also profoundly marked the history of Western Europe."[1]

The Church

Charlemagne's deep belief in the Christian faith also profoundly marked the history of Western Europe. Christianity had been widespread throughout Europe for centuries before the Frankish king's time, but he felt a moral obligation to broaden its reach by converting non-Christian, or pagan, tribes within his lands to it—sometimes forcefully.

His beliefs led Charlemagne to form alliances with the most important religious leaders of the day, strengthening a lasting union between religion and government—that is, between church and state. This bond pushed to a new level the power of the Christian Church, and in time the teachings and practices of the church permeated virtually all aspects of public policy, political strategy, and daily life.

In later centuries western Christianity split into two major halves; the older half became known as Roman Catholicism and the younger as Protestantism. During the Middle Ages, however, it was a single entity, usually referred to in history books as Christianity or simply the church.

Christendom

Christianity became such a prevalent and strong force that a new term emerged to link together the kingdoms of Europe: Christendom. This word reflects the fact that many of the kingdoms across the continent, including Charlemagne's, had at least one thing in common: a shared religion.

For most of the early medieval period, the term *Europe* was not used. However, to a large degree *Christendom* served the same purpose. Historian J.M. Roberts comments, "A shorthand way of describing what happened . . . after the end of the old Roman Empire in the west is to say that half [of] Christendom then turned into Europe."[2]

Together with Islamic society—which dominated the Middle East and was making steady inroads in Europe—the rise of Christianity profoundly defined the early medieval era. Historian Colin McEvedy argues that the two religions were the era's single most defining factors. He comments, "The theme of the medieval centuries is not the decline and fall of the Roman Empire but the emergence of Islam and western Christendom."[3]

The teachings of Saint Paul (pictured in this fourteenth-century painting) had a profound influence on the early Christian church—both through his work as a missionary to spread the Gospel and through his writing of a large portion of the New Testament.

A Framework for Understanding the Past

The importance of the church notwithstanding, another phenomenon that formed the essence of the early Middle Ages was feudalism. Feudalism was a social, political, and economic structure that, like religion, permeated virtually every aspect of life. Based on Europe's agricultural economy, feudalism formed a social hierarchy that separated social classes but, at the same time, bound them together with ties of obligation, loyalty, and service.

Feudalism, religion, and the transition from empire to kingdoms were the primary characteristics of the early Middle Ages. Although there is debate about when this era ended, the start of the religious wars called the Crusades in 1096 is often used to mark the end of the early Middle Ages.

Many historians stress, however, that such dates are only convenient markers. For this era (or any other, for that matter) a number of milestones could serve equally well as markers for beginning and ending points. Furthermore, factors such as feudalism and Christianity arrived in different regions at different times, and with different consequences.

In short, history is never divided into neat sections with clear beginnings and endings. Using only dates to separate eras is not enough. Historian Peter S. Wells comments, "Too often, modern researchers lost sight of the fact that these fixed points are intended only to provide a framework for understanding peoples of the past, not real breaks in the social or cultural development of early Europeans."[4]

Nonetheless, the early medieval era obviously began somewhere. The fall of the Western Roman Empire is an excellent reference point for launching its story.

Chapter 1

What Events Led to the Early Middle Ages?

The Roman Empire, at its height in the second century AD, was one of the most literate and sophisticated cultures of its time, and indeed in world history. For centuries it ruled not only much of Europe but also large portions of North Africa and Asia Minor. Edward Gibbon, an eighteenth-century English writer, was the author of a classic work on this imperial realm, *The History of the Decline and Fall of the Roman Empire*. Gibbon (who apparently did not take into consideration other sophisticated civilizations of the time, such as that of China) noted:

> In the second century of the Christian era, the empire of Rome comprehended the fairest part of the earth, and the most civilised portion of mankind. The frontiers of that extensive monarchy were guarded by ancient renown and disciplined valour. The . . . influence of law and manners had gradually cemented the union of the provinces. Their peaceful inhabitants enjoyed and abused the advantages of wealth and luxury. The image of a free constitution [a set of laws] was preserved with decent reverence.[5]

From their headquarters in Rome, the empire's rulers relentlessly pushed into new lands, sending armies and administrators to every corner. Organized and powerful, the Romans built bustling cities, defensive structures, and roughly 50,000 miles (80,000km) of roads throughout their empire. The construction work of the Romans was so sturdy that remnants of it can still be seen, in some cases as many as 2,000 years after the structures were originally built.

In this way Rome extended its highly developed language, customs, arts, and government, bringing together (to varying degrees) countless diverse tribes of people. At its peak, the Roman Empire covered some 2.2 million square miles (5.7 million sq. km). Population estimates vary widely, from 65 million to 130 million—somewhere between 20 and 40 percent of the world's inhabitants. The empire's success thus made it the greatest power on earth between the first and fifth centuries AD.

In short, the Roman Empire was built solidly and ran smoothly. Historian Colin McEvedy comments: "The frontiers were secure, the civil order largely unchallenged, and the people free to pursue the arts of peace. There were black spots: the institution of slavery [and] the unhappy circumstances of Egypt [which the Romans plundered] and Palestine [which Rome destroyed]. But by and large the *pax Romana* [Roman peace] worked."[6]

Two Halves of the Empire

The solidity of the Roman Empire as a whole began its long decline in 285, when Emperor Diocletian split his vast territory into two semi-independent sections. The split came about for several reasons. The empire had grown too large to govern from one capital, there was a high turnover of rulers, the expense of maintaining the region was enormous, and monetary inflation was out of control. The Western Roman Empire encompassed modern-day England, France, Germany, Spain, and other nations. The Eastern Roman Empire, meanwhile, included territory in the Middle East, North Africa, and what is now Turkey.

There were many differences between the two. One was economic. The Western Empire's treasury was stretched to its limits because of the expense of maintaining its borders. By contrast, the Eastern Empire, with its lucrative trade links to Africa and Asia, was far richer.

The division between the halves proved to be a dramatic turning point for the empire. This widening rift became even more obvious in 330 after Emperor Constantine, one of Diocletian's successors, renamed the ancient city of Byzantium as Constantinople in his own honor and made it the capital of the Eastern Empire. (Today this city is known as Istanbul.) Historian J.M. Roberts writes: "Constantine's acts . . . confirmed the cultural division of east and west. He made it easier still for them to drift apart. The more populous east could feed itself and raise more taxes and recruits; the west grew poorer, its towns slipping to decline. . . . Gradually Constantinople came to rival Rome and even surpass it."[7]

The Barbarians

By the beginning of the fifth century, the western half of the Roman Empire was seriously beginning to weaken. The most significant reason for this was the inability of the once-mighty Roman army to stop fierce assaults of invaders from beyond the borders of its territory.

Romans called these invaders "barbarians" (a name taken from the Latin word for any people living outside Roman-held territory). Many such tribes plagued the Romans; among the most powerful were the Goths and Vandals from what is now Germany; the Alans, Magyars, and Huns from central Europe; and the Vikings from the Scandinavian regions of the far north.

These and other barbarians—whether they wanted to acquire Roman land or simply keep what they already had—regularly brought panic and terror to the inhabitants of the Roman Empire's fringes. They were for the most part ferocious warriors with a reputation for ruthlessness. One observer of the time, a clergyman named Photius, wrote that the raiders were "barbarous, nomadic, armed with arrogance, unwatched, unchallenged, leaderless . . . boldly thrusting their sword through persons of every age and sex."[8]

Many other observers in other parts of the empire had similar reactions. Another member of the clergy, a monk in England, wrote in the aftermath of one barbarian attack that "there is no road, there is no place, where the ground is not strewn with corpses."[9] And a Roman historian of the time, Ammianus Marcellinus, wrote that the Huns "are not subject to the authority of any king, but break through any obstacle in their path under the improvised command of their chief men."[10] Of course, these witnesses, as Roman citizens, were understandably biased, but since virtually no barbarian tribe kept records, nothing exists of their point of view.

Refusing to Be Enslaved or Governed

As might be expected, the onslaught of the invaders had several dramatic repercussions for the Romans. For one thing, the costs associated with defending the border regions of Rome's empire skyrocketed. For another, vast numbers of barbarians who were not warriors—typically the families of warriors—followed in the wake of successful invasions, settling in newly acquired lands and chipping away at the Roman realm.

Historians often call this era the great migration period, because so many people moved from one region to another. There were several reasons for this extensive wandering (including serious climatic changes), but a major one was the desire to settle in land newly taken or taken back from the Romans.

The cultures and practices of these tribes varied considerably. Some groups chose to cooperate with Roman rule, paying taxes in exchange for the right to live and farm on what was officially Roman land. Others were more warlike, simply invading and overrunning existing rule.

Some were pagans—that is, not Christians, which the subjects of the Roman Empire officially were by this time. Other tribes, meanwhile, were relatively recent converts to Christianity, although they often practiced a form of the religion that was in conflict with Roman beliefs.

Not all of the land claimed by invaders was new territory to the barbarians, of course. Some of these tribes had been ousted from their native homes by previous Roman administrations. Understandably, they were eager to reclaim land that they believed was rightfully theirs. The

The Spread of Christianity in the Roman Empire

The close connection between religion and politics began long before the medieval era. In the case of European Christianity, it can be traced to the days of the Romans, as missionaries spread Christianity from its origin in the Middle East into the Mediterranean region and beyond. This process was by no means smooth; resistance to the new religion within the empire and among the barbarian tribes outside it was frequently passionate to the point of violence.

Such violence led, in some cases, to incidences of martyrdom, when Roman leaders persecuted Christians—people who were so dedicated to their religion that they would rather die than deny that devotion. The last large-scale incidences of discrimination against Christians took place early in the fourth century, when Christians who refused to pray to the Roman gods were imprisoned, tortured, and executed. However, cases of extreme persecution grew increasingly rare after the first centuries of the Middle Ages. (This was not true for other religions. Notably, Jews were regularly and severely persecuted during this period.)

After the persecution against it declined, Christianity began steadily gaining ground. Many Roman subjects and members of barbarian tribes found the new religion appealing and found its highly organized structure admirable. Increasingly, these tribes left their pagan (non-Christian) beliefs behind. McEvedy comments:

> The sudden collapse of the older [religious] order is not really surprising. Paganism had never been more than a rag-bag of local cults and superstitions; it had few consistencies and no organization at all. By contrast, the Christian church had a message that many people wanted to hear, and the means of delivering it round the Mediterranean world.

Colin McEvedy, *The New Penguin Atlas of Medieval History*. New York: Penguin, 1992, p. 22.

Romans fought hard to retain the empire's borders, but the invaders could be merciless as well; a Roman observer of the time noted that one tribe, the Slavs, "refus[ed] to be enslaved or governed, bearing readily heat, cold, rain, nakedness, and scarcity of provisions."[11]

The Empire Falls

As the empire steadily weakened under this onslaught, the barbarian tribes became bolder, attacking hard, fast, and, often, successfully. The single most significant invasion of this period was the storming and occupation in 410 of the capital city itself by a Germanic tribe of warriors called the Visigoths.

This devastating blow, the sack of Rome, was a stunning defeat. It was the first time in 800 years that Rome had suffered a successful direct invasion, and it shook both halves of the empire. A famous priest, Jerome (later Saint Jerome), wrote of the event:

> I shudder when I think of the calamities of our time. For twenty years the blood of Romans has been shed daily between Constantinople and the Alps. . . . These regions have been sacked and pillaged by Goths and Alans, Huns and Vandals. How many noble and virtuous women have been made the sport of these beasts! . . . The Roman world is falling [and] Rome's army, once the lord of the world, trembles today at the sight of the foe.[12]

Although the Eastern Roman Empire narrowly survived the assaults on its land, the western half could not. This was due in part to the strain on the less affluent Western Empire's economy, but the exact reasons remain unclear even to experts today. Historian Chris Wickham comments, "Why the Roman Empire vanished in the West and not in the East is a problem that has perplexed generations of scholars, and will continue to do so."[13]

After a long period of decline, the Western Empire's collapse finally came. In 476 Romulus Augustus, the young and incompetent emperor, was forced to abdicate his throne. Odoacer, the ruler of the Kingdom

Huns launch a ferocious assault against their enemy. The Huns were just one of several "barbarian" tribes who challenged the Roman Empire's hold on its western territories beginning in the fifth century.

of Italy (today northern Italy), took his place and assumed control over much of the former Roman territory.

However, he did not rule over all of the empire. Rather, the once mighty and highly organized Roman Empire descended into increasing chaos and disintegration. Gibbon noted, "The union of the Roman empire was dissolved; its genius was humbled in the dust; and armies of unknown barbarians, issuing from the frozen regions of the North, had established their victorious reign over the fairest provinces of Europe and Africa."[14] For all intents and purposes, the Middle Ages had begun.

Odoacer, the First Barbarian King

Odoacer, the first barbarian king of what had been the Western Roman Empire, was born in what is now Germany in about 434. He was born into one of the region's barbarian tribes, perhaps the Scyrri.

As a young man, Odoacer was conscripted into the Roman army. A Christian and probably illiterate, he rose in the ranks of the military. When Emperor Orestes refused the demands of a group of barbarian warriors to give them one-third of Italy, Odoacer sided with them and betrayed Orestes, in return asking for the throne.

The rebels succeeded in toppling the throne, which was now held by Orestes's teenage son, Romulus Augustus. In August 476 Odoacer captured the young ruler and forced him to abdicate and go into exile; his father and uncle, however, were slaughtered.

Odoacer reigned for 13 years. Little more is known about him, although his rule apparently benefited the ruling classes. Odoacer was betrayed by Theodoric, the leader of a barbarian tribe, the Ostrogoths. Theodoric waged war on Odoacer and then convinced him to accept a peace treaty ensuring that they would rule together. At a banquet celebrating that agreement, Theodoric killed his rival and took the throne for himself.

The Great Migration Continues

The Roman lands were now under the control of many regional warlords, who controlled their own small, disjointed, independent, and loosely structured kingdoms. The most powerful of these included the Ostrogoths (who controlled what is now Italy), the Visigoths (in what is now Spain and Portugal), the Franks and Burgundians (who controlled what is now France and western Germany), and the Angles and the Saxons (in what is now England).

As these barbarian tribes solidified their power in specific regions, huge numbers of people continued to travel as the great migration period continued. By 500, for example, the Visigoths had thoroughly settled large parts of what are now France, Spain, and Portugal.

Lawlessness

Long after the empire finally collapsed, the "petty kings"—that is, the rulers of the region's many small territories—continued to invade each other's territory, claiming the land as their own. As control of a given region shifted, the cultural makeup of the people living there shifted as well. Some decided to stay and continue living under their new leaders. Typically, this meant acquiring new languages and customs, although some regions, notably in the Italian Peninsula and the Iberian Peninsula (modern-day Spain and Portugal), were able to retain much of their old, Roman-influenced ways.

Meanwhile, as the continent fractured politically, Europe as a whole was entering a grim period. For one thing, the mortality rate skyrocketed, due to widespread famine and epidemics of disease. Europe's population dropped significantly during the years after the end of Roman rule, declining from an estimated 45 million to about 36 million.

Furthermore, without the highly developed organization the Romans had brought, there were no longer any clear borders or laws. Poverty and civic disorder became commonplace. Crucial elements of Roman civilization, such as literacy, learning, art, and the manufacture of goods, died out. Libraries, public baths, roads, stone buildings, and other amenities—all once features of Roman life—fell into disrepair or disappeared altogether. Little, if anything, was done to replace them.

The Near End of Travel and Commerce

During this period, the ability to travel from one region to another steeply declined. One reason was that the sturdy roads built by the Romans deteriorated. Another was that the withdrawal of Roman military

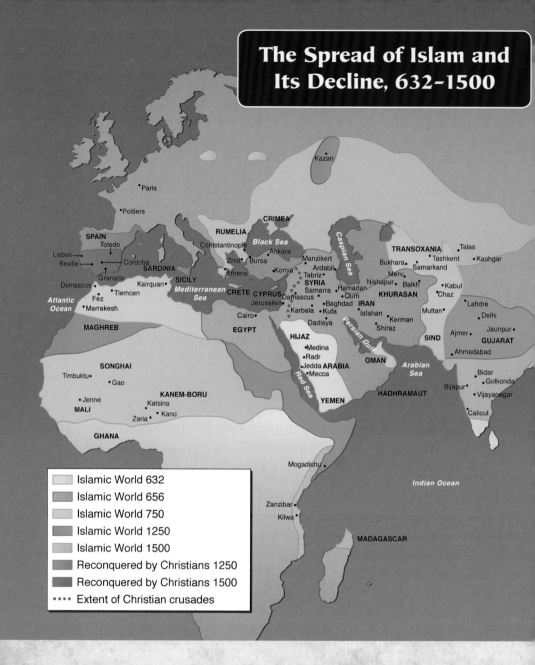

The Spread of Islam and Its Decline, 632–1500

Kazan

Paris

Poitiers

CRIMEA

RUMELIA

SPAIN

Toledo

Black Sea

Contstantinople

Ankara

TRANSOXANIA

Talas

Lisbon

Cordoba

Zmit

Bursa

Manzikert

Bukhara

Tashkent

Kashgar

Seville

Konya

Ardabil

Samarkand

Damascus

Granada

SARDINIA

SICILY

Athens

Tabriz

Merv

Nishapur

Balkh

Kabul

Fez

Kairquan

Mediterranean Sea

CRETE

CYPRUS

Damascus

Samarra

Hamadan

KHURASAN

Chaz

Atlantic Ocean

Tlemcen

SYRIA

Qum

IRAN

Lahdre

Marrakesh

Jerusalem

Baghdad

Isfahan

Kerman

Multan

Delhi

Cairo

Karbala

Kufa

Dadisya

Shiraz

Ajmer

Jaunpur

MAGHREB

EGYPT

HIJAZ

SIND

GUJARAT

Medina

Ahmadabad

Radr

OMAN

Jedda

ARABIA

Arabian Sea

Bidar

SONGHAI

Mecca

Golkonda

Timbuktu

Gao

KANEM-BORU

Bijapur

Vijayanagar

Jenne

Katsina

HADHRAMAUT

YEMEN

Calicut

MALI

Zaria

Kano

GHANA

Mogadishu

Indian Ocean

	Islamic World 632
	Islamic World 656
	Islamic World 750
	Islamic World 1250
	Islamic World 1500
	Reconquered by Christians 1250
	Reconquered by Christians 1500
····	Extent of Christian crusades

Zanzibar

Kilwa

MADAGASCAR

protection meant that bandits could openly prey along travel routes. Even under the best of circumstances, travel had been difficult, slow, and cumbersome. Now, it was nearly impossible.

This situation would continue for centuries. In fact, even after political borders opened up, travel was not easily undertaken. There were remarkably few significant innovations in land-based travel or communication until the Industrial Revolution of the nineteenth century.

Roberts notes, "Between the age of the [Roman] Caesars and that of the steam railway there was [virtually] no increase in the speed with which messages and goods could be sent overland in Europe."[15]

Travel was essential, of course, for all but the most localized forms of trade and business. Trade within and among nations fell as the ease of travel declined, and the well-being of the region's inhabitants declined as well. Rival tribes and kingdoms cut each other off from crucial trade routes and thus blocked access to grain, spices, preservatives, perfumes, dyes, and other valuable items from Africa and Asia. Some aspects of European manufacturing that relied on trade outside of the immediate area, such as the making of fine pottery, virtually disappeared. Instead, communities made their own crude products.

This situation dramatically limited the lives of everyday people. Peter S. Wells comments, "Without Roman control of the seas and overland highways, trade collapsed and communities became cut off from the larger world."[16] It was an unusual event indeed when a person ventured even briefly beyond the immediate area of his or her own farm or village.

The East Hangs On

The former Western Roman Empire continued to fracture and sink into an increasing darkness. However, the eastern half of the Roman Empire managed to hold on to most of its culture and at least some of its territories. But over the next several centuries, it faced serious threats of its own from a variety of invaders.

The most serious of these were highly organized armies from lands to the east. These warriors came from different cultures, but they shared a relatively new religion called Islam. Very quickly, Islamic forces succeeded in controlling vast amounts of former Roman territory in what are now Syria, Egypt, North Africa, and parts of Europe near the Mediterranean Sea, including the Iberian Peninsula (today's Spain and Portugal). McEvedy comments, "Within twenty years of the Prophet's [Muhammad's] death [in 632], the Arabs had created an empire to rival Rome's."[17]

The Birth of Islam

The religion of Islam was founded in the early seventh century by Muhammad, a man believed by Muslims to be a holy prophet. Born in 570 in the city of Mecca (in today's Saudi Arabia), Muhammad began teaching his faith, according to Muslim beliefs, after hearing the voice of the angel Gabriel in the year 610. Islam's holiest book, the Koran, spells out Muhammad's beliefs, in particular a faith in the one true God, Allah.

After Muhammad died in 632, his followers—composed of tribes from throughout Arabia—continued to spread his message. A combination of powerful military forces, extensive trading, and widespread settlement led to the occupation of new lands and the religious conversion of the inhabitants of those lands.

Within 100 years of Muhammad's death, Islam controlled nearly half of what was then the known world. Its vast empire reached from the Strait of Gibraltar to the Himalayan Mountains and included North and West Africa, the Middle East, Persia, and the Iberian Peninsula (modern Spain and Portugal). This empire was among the largest ever seen, more extensive even than the Roman Empire at its height.

The Arabs set their sights on expanding the lands under their control. Notably, they crossed from North Africa into the Iberian Peninsula, as well as parts of southern Italy. They then used this territory as a staging point for launching eastward attacks.

During this period, still other threats to the Eastern Empire came from different directions. Among the strongest of the invading tribes were the Avars, descendants of the fearsome Mongolian Empire, which had once covered central and southern Asia, Siberia, India, and other lands. The Avars now controlled large portions of central and eastern Europe. By the end of the 600s, as a result of incursions by the Avars, Muslims, and others, the Eastern Roman Empire controlled only small pockets of its once huge territory.

Political Chaos

As the Eastern Empire struggled with its own problems, Western Europe's political structure remained chaotic. With little ability to band together defensively, the barbarian tribes that had filled the void left by the Romans continued to control only their own relatively small territories—a collection of localized rival societies that fiercely protected their own (and often conflicting) customs, languages, and habits.

Despite their independent status, Europe's petty kingdoms did sometimes band together for certain purposes. Typically, these alliances were forged for simple gain—two states might form a partnership, for instance, to invade a third. Another reason for creating an alliance concerned the protection—or gain—of trade routes. Controlling a particular mountain pass or a certain seaway, for example, might mean the difference between prosperity and starvation for a tribe.

These small kingdoms, considered together, formed a complex web of intrigue and shifting loyalties. As a result, borders and populations were fluid and changeable—and thus were a ready source of conflict. Roberts summarizes this state of affairs simply: "Medieval boundaries did not mean what they mean today."[18] However, this volatile and disorganized situation would, in time, coalesce into something new.

Chapter 2

The Rise of Kingdoms

O ut of the many petty kingdoms that filled the void left by the Roman Empire's collapse, one stood out far above the others. The Frankish Empire, as it was called, came closer than any other entity in medieval times to creating a unified empire—something that had been impossible in the centuries immediately after Rome fell. The political and social reforms created and enforced by Charlemagne, the Frankish Empire's greatest leader, became cornerstones in the development of virtually every future European state. Even after this realm dissolved, its physical boundaries became the framework for much of Europe's future political geography.

England

The Frankish land may have been the largest and most influential kingdom to evolve in Europe during these years, but it was not the only one. One example of another developing region was England. This island was originally made up of tribes such as the Celts. Many of these tribes had been under Roman rule. (A notable exception was a tribe called the Picts, who lived in what is now Scotland; they were fierce warriors who managed to keep the Romans at bay.)

When the Roman Empire fell, its forces withdrew from England. The island then became the target of regular invasions by Germanic tribes from the mainland, including the Jutes, the Angles, and the Saxons. The natives were only partially successful at keeping these outsiders from invading, and a steady stream of immigrants settled there.

Despite the chaos and hostility this created, the tribes of England, and to an extent the outsiders who had settled there, were able to form several small kingdoms, the most prominent being Northumbria, Mercia, Kent, East Anglia, Essex, Sussex, and Wessex.

Power continued to shift between invaders and England's small kingdoms. One group of outsiders was an alliance of Scandinavians known as the Vikings. They established themselves on the far northern islands of Scotland and used them to conduct raids along the English coast. A charismatic ruler of Wessex in the mid- to late-ninth century, Alfred the Great, was able to fend them off to a degree, but they remained an aggressive presence and settled in several regions of the island.

Trading by Ship

The Vikings and other barbarian tribes of northern Europe were able to plunder—and eventually trade with—other lands because they had always been seagoing peoples. They developed a number of innovations, new to Europe, that gave them advantages over other regions. The first vessels that took Anglo-Saxon warriors in raids to England, for instance, were powered by ranks of 30 to 40 oarsmen per boat.

Then, around the eighth century, the northern barbarians developed their own versions of sailing ships. These sailboats were a major technological advance. They allowed warriors to venture much farther from shore than previously. As a result, their trading and plundering abilities grew much more extensive. Although the Scandinavians traded in furs, textiles, food, and other products, their main products were slaves captured in battle. In return they wanted precious commodities such as gold, silver, and silk.

In time, however, Alfred gained the upper hand over both the raiders and the island's other kingdoms, beginning the process of unifying the island under one ruler. (Historians acknowledge Alfred's grandson, Aethelstan, as the first king to unite England, in 927.) Alfred is considered so important to the development of England that he is the only king of that nation to have been honored with "the Great" after his name.

The seagoing people known as the Vikings developed sophisticated sailing ships that carried them far from Scandinavian shores and contributed to shifting alliances and power struggles in England and elsewhere. An eighth-century Viking ship departs Norway in this illustration.

The Franks

Despite its great importance in later years, however, England was at the time a relatively obscure part of the world. The most influential force in Europe, by far, was the Frankish Empire. At its peak, in about 800, the Frankish Empire encompassed a significant part of the European continent. Its borders stretched from what is now northern Spain eastward to what is now Austria, including almost all of today's France, the Low Countries, Germany, and northern Italy. Population figures for this realm are speculative, but estimates put the number of people living within the Frankish Empire at its height at 15 million—perhaps half of the total population of Europe.

As the name suggests, the monarchy arose from a people called the Franks. The Franks, in turn, had evolved from a loose coalition of cultures called the Germanic tribes in the regions around the Rhine Valley of modern-day Germany. These barbarian tribes had been raiding regions of the Roman Empire as early as the middle of the third century.

As the Roman realm dissolved, the dominant Germanic tribe, the Salians, succeeded by the late fifth century in uniting with the others. This group collectively was known as the Merovingians. In time the Merovingians evolved into another group of people: the Franks.

Clovis and His Sons

The most influential of the Merovingian kings was Clovis, who fought a bloody war with rival leaders to win the throne in about 482. Clovis pushed his kingdom into northern Gaul (part of France today) and gave it a different name: Neustria, or "New Land," to differentiate it from the original Merovingian territory, which was called Austrasia ("Eastern Land").

Clovis continued to expand his realm. In the late fifth and early sixth centuries, he conquered a group of tribes that collectively were called the Alemanni, thus gaining vast amounts of land along the upper Rhine River (in modern-day Germany), Brittany (in what is now northwestern France), and Aquitaine (southwestern France).

When Clovis died in 511, his four sons assumed control. This was in keeping with a long-standing tradition among many cultures: that of rulers succeeding each other in a hereditary line, passing the crown from brother to brother, or father to son or, less commonly, a sister or daughter.

In the case of Clovis, however, this tradition of hereditary succession was a political disaster. Rather than maintaining a unified and extensive kingdom with a single ruler (or corulers who could cooperate), Clovis's sons frequently fought with each other. This lack of central control led to chaos, making it easier for barbarian tribes to invade and giving outlying regions the opportunity to rebel.

As a result, the kingdom shrank significantly during this time. As Clovis's sons aged and died, their fragile empire gradually evolved into three loosely allied sections: Neustria, Austrasia, and Burgundy (part of modern-day France and Switzerland).

Charlemagne

In the years around 685, the ruler of Austrasia, Pépin of Herstal, was able to unify these realms into one territory. His son Charles Martel then took over and became the first ruler of a new line of kings, the Carolingian dynasty. (The name comes from Charles's Latin name, Carolus.) This succession of kings, which lasted into the late 900s, can be considered the major link between the fracturing of Europe and the long period of relative economic and political cohesion that came later. Historian Geoffrey Barraclough writes, "Not surprisingly, most historians have seen the establishment of the Carolingian empire as 'the central figure' of European history between the fall of the Roman empire in the west and the emergence of the feudal monarchies."[19]

Charles and his son, Pépin the Short, continued to wage war with their neighbors. They successfully reunited much of Clovis's empire and held off invaders. Control then passed to Charles's sons, Charles and Carloman, who ruled together. When Carloman died in 771, the empire went to Charles, soon known by a grander name: Charlemagne, or Charles the Great.

In many respects Charlemagne was the essence of the Middle Ages. His kingdom was the framework for the nations of modern-day Europe. McEvedy comments, "Charlemagne's empire did not, of course, have much to do with the old Roman Empire; it didn't even have much resemblance to it geographically. However, the order he imposed on western Europe does represent a new base-line."[20]

The king was, first of all, responsible for expanding the Frankish Empire to its greatest extent and maintaining its unity. But that is not the only reason he was called Charles the Great. He also sponsored far-reaching laws and reforms, based on ancient Roman and Greek culture, that spread across much of the continent. Furthermore, he forged a close bond with the Christian Church, ensuring a continuing connection between religion and politics.

Charlemagne was also warlike. In nearly 50 years as ruler, Charlemagne mounted about 60 military campaigns. For half of them, he personally led the way, wielding his legendary sword Joyeuse. This dual role as a warrior-king was a powerful continuation of a grand and ancient tradition.

Charlemagne's Empire

NORSE

SWEDES

SCOTS DANES

Baltic Sea

North Sea

ANGLES AND SAXONS

Aachen SAXONY

WILZIANS

SORBS SLAVS

AUSTRASIA

Paris

CZECHS

NORDGAU

MORAVIANS

BRITTANY NEUSTRIA

BAVARIA

AVARS

CARINTHIA

BURGUNDY Venice

ALLEMANNIA

CROATS

North Atlantic Ocean

AQUITAINE

LOMBARDY

PAPAL STATES

BYZANTINE EMPIRE

SPOLETO

KINGDOM OF ASTURIUS

CORSICA

Rome

Barcelona

SARDINIA

SICILY

DUCHY OF BENEVENTO

MUSLIM TERRITORY

BALLEARIC ISLANDS

Mediterranean Sea

	Charlemagne's empire in 771
	Areas added after 771
★	Capital

MUSLIM TERRITORY

The Carolingian Renaissance

Throughout his many conquests, Charlemagne was responsible for thousands of deaths, brutal subjugation of the populations he conquered, and massive plundering of treasure. On the other hand, the wealth from these conquests gave Charlemagne the opportunity to create a positive and lasting legacy: the flowering of culture known as the Carolingian

Charlemagne has often been depicted in paintings, sculptures, and writing. Of course, descriptions of him might be exaggerated or overly flattering. Nonetheless, they do provide a glimpse of the man. Apparently, he was unusually tall, especially for an age when people were much smaller than today. He was charismatic and intense in manner. Einhard, a cleric of the king's court who wrote a biography of him, had this to say: "He was six feet four inches tall, and built to scale. He had beautiful white hair, animated eyes, a powerful nose . . . a presence always stately and dignified. He was temperate in eating and drinking, abominated drunkenness, and kept in good health despite every exposure and hardship."

Except for ceremonial occasions, he wore traditional Frankish clothes: a linen shirt and breeches, tunic, and a cloak or fur coat in winter. He carried his sword with him at all times, and on ceremonial occasions wore a jewel-encrusted saber.

Peter S. Wells, *Barbarians to Angels: The Dark Ages Reconsidered*. New York: Norton, 2008, p. 186.

Renaissance. (The term *Renaissance*, meaning a rebirth, would also be used for the period of European history that followed the Middle Ages.)

The Carolingian Renaissance saw dramatic reforms and innovations in many areas of society, including education, economics, and culture. These reforms represented a revival of inquiry, human values, and creative energy. Such qualities, once a major part of Roman life, had lain dormant in Europe for centuries but were now beginning to blossom.

The center of the Carolingian Renaissance was the royal capital of Aachen, on what is now the western border of Germany. Here, the king assembled scholars and religious leaders from his realm and beyond.

Through them, the Frankish Empire became a haven of enlightened thought and scholarship in what otherwise was often a world of brutality, chaos, and ignorance.

Economic Reforms

One important reform Charlemagne instigated was the development of an improved system of money, a reform that had begun with Pépin. This aspect of economic reform had far-reaching results; it served as the basis for monetary systems that are still in use today.

One facet of Charlemagne's new system of managing his kingdom's money was to abandon the gold standard—that is, the use of a standard measure of gold as a basis for minting coins. In its place the ruler established a new measurement of money, the *livre carolinienne*, based on silver.

In the short term this was necessary because of a scarcity of gold in the kingdom; the growing Islamic empire was blocking trade routes leading to sources of the metal. In the long term the reform proved extremely useful. It unified the confusing and contradictory kinds of currencies that had been used within the Frankish realm. This, in turn, simplified and expanded the kingdom's ability to conduct trade and commerce.

Another of Charlemagne's economic reforms was to improve business practices. For instance, the king passed laws establishing standards for bookkeeping, charging interest, and price controls. All of these helped simplify commerce and minimize corruption.

Supporting Learning

Charlemagne set an example for his subjects by hiring tutors for himself. Furthermore, he educated his children and grandchildren—even the girls, which was unusual for that time. And he supported education elsewhere by increasing the number of church-run schools. The Frankish king also gave clergy leaders a number of educational responsibilities beyond daily instruction. Among these were the creation of textbooks

Charlemagne brutally subjugated the populations he conquered and plundered their treasures but at the same, under his reign, innovations in economics and education contributed to the development of European civilization.

and a standardized curriculum. He also sponsored the creation of Carolingian minuscule, a form of writing based on the Roman alphabet that was an important step forward in the ability to communicate.

Furthermore, Carolingian scholars created a standardized version of Latin that allowed the addition of new words but kept its grammatical rules. This so-called Medieval Latin remained the common language among educated people across Europe for hundreds of years. It radically improved communication by providing a common tongue for the diverse cultures in the kingdom, and it became the basis for the Romance languages of modern times.

The Next Generation

Charlemagne's rule could not last forever. Beginning in about 780, when he was in his late thirties, he began to pass authority to the next generation.

Charlemagne made arrangements to divide his realm between two of his sons, Carloman and Louis the Pious. (The king reportedly had 17 children by several wives and mistresses, although not all lived to adulthood.)

Carloman was appointed king of Italy and assumed a new name: Pépin the Short. Louis, meanwhile, became king of Aquitaine and heir to the throne. In 813 Louis was named co-emperor with his father. Early in 814 Charlemagne fell ill with pleurisy, a respiratory disease, and passed away in late January.

The great king was buried in Aachen Cathedral. He was 72 years old, had reigned for 46 years, and was widely mourned. An anonymous monk of Bobbio, in what is now northern Italy, summed up the feelings of many (perhaps exaggerating a little) when he lamented:

> From the lands where the sun rises to western shores, people are crying and wailing . . . the Franks, the Romans, all Christians, are stung with mourning and great worry. . . . The young and old, glorious nobles, all lament the loss of their Caesar. . . . The world laments the death of Charles. . . . O Christ, you who govern the heavenly host, grant a peaceful place to Charles in your kingdom. Alas for miserable me.[21]

After Charlemagne

The new king, Louis the Pious, as his name suggests, was deeply religious, and this faith became a cornerstone of his reign. Like his father before him, Louis saw himself as the leader of a unified land of Christians. Father and son both recognized the political advantage of binding otherwise disparate tribes together in the name of a shared religion.

In the opinion of many historians, Louis was a competent ruler. Despite his best efforts, however, the Frankish government began to unravel during his reign. This was due to a number of problematic situations, some of them beyond the king's power to solve. Notable among them was a successful revolt for independence in the small portion of Spain that was part of the Frankish lands. Louis also was unable to completely stop the continued attacks on his empire's vulnerable edges by outside raiders.

Meanwhile, the question of succession came up again. Louis the Pious and his first wife, Ermingarde, had three sons: Pépin, Lothair, and Louis (later called Louis the German). Looking ahead to the day one of them would rule, the siblings maintained an uneasy truce for years.

However, in 818 Ermingarde died, and Louis the Pious remarried, to a woman named Judith. In 823 Judith gave birth to another son, Charles (later called Charles the Bald). This further complicated an already complex situation. Louis the Pious tried to share land equitably among his older sons and his new one. However, conflict within the royal family about succession led to open revolt by the older brothers against their father.

The Kingdom Splits

In 833 the siblings and their supporters forced Louis the Pious to abdicate briefly. He eventually managed to regain the throne, which he held until his death in 840. At that point the three living brothers (Pépin had died in 838) fought among themselves again. Civil war broke out among the various supporters of the brothers and threatened to destroy the entire empire. Eventually, the three contentious brothers reached an agreement in 843 with a compromise that became known as the Treaty of Verdun.

The treaty split the Frankish Empire into three portions that were together called Francia. The eldest surviving son became Lothair I, ruling what became Middle Francia, an area that made up much of what is now northern Italy and portions of central Europe. Louis the German, the second son, became king of East Francia, the bulk of which formed what is now Austria, Switzerland, and Germany. Meanwhile, the third son, Charles the Bald, presided over West Francia. This region primarily covered much of modern-day southern and western France.

The division marked a dramatic turning point in the history of the Frankish realm. A once-unified empire was now fractured into several lands with shifting allegiances, uncertain borders, and frequent strife. In essence it marked a return to the chaotic political situation that had existed before Charlemagne.

The Byzantine Empire

EUROPE

Black Sea

Ravenna
Constantinople

ITALY
Rome

SPAIN

Cordova

Athens

ASIA

Carthage

Mediterranean Sea

Alexandria

AFRICA

EGYPT

AD 476
AD 565

The ill effects of the split grew more pronounced with the next genera-tions of rulers, who divided the land into even smaller pieces. For exam-ple, Lothair's three sons divided their father's kingdom between them into three separate regions. This process of continued division steadily weak-ened the power of what could have remained a single mighty kingdom.

The Carolingian dynasty continued to decline and finally ended with the death of Charlemagne's great-grandson, Charles the Fat, in 888. The empire that Charlemagne had unified and strengthened was gone, now replaced by what it had once been—a decentralized array of kingdoms. Barraclough comments, "The empire . . . had no future; it simply petered out."[22]

The Byzantine Empire

Meanwhile, another significant realm with a long and noble his-tory was thriving in eastern Europe, North Africa, the Middle East,

The Most Beautiful Cathedral

One of the great achievements of the Byzantine ruler Justinian I was the construction during his reign of the magnificent Hagia Sophia cathedral in Constantinople, Byzantium's capital. Hagia Sophia is still considered one of the most beautiful buildings in the world. The power of its beauty is illustrated by a story about a visit to Constantinople by representatives of Prince Vladimir of Kiev, in what is now Ukraine.

Vladimir wanted to convert his realm to Christianity, but he was not sure which branch of the church appealed to him the most: the western branch or the Orthodox branch centered in Constantinople. While exploring this question, the ruler sent a delegation to the Byzantine capital in 987 and ordered them to report back. The delegation went to Constantinople and saw Justinian's Hagia Sophia and, on its return to Kiev, told Vladimir, "We knew not whether we were in heaven or on earth. We can never forget that beauty." According to tradition, that was enough to convince Vladimir, and he chose the Orthodox faith.

Quoted in Colin McEvedy, *The New Penguin Atlas of Medieval History*. New York: Penguin, 1992, p. 54.

and Asia Minor. This was the Byzantine Empire, which had evolved from the Eastern Roman Empire. Its roots were primarily in Greek culture, and its political and religious center was still in Constantinople.

One of the most important of the Byzantine rulers was Justinian I, who assumed the throne in 527. Among other achievements, he expanded the empire, brought it to a peak of prosperity, and developed major legal reforms. The ruler was also instrumental in his empire's development of a well-defined and unique culture. J.M.

Roberts writes, "After [Justinian], Byzantine civilization was really distinct from Roman."[23]

One aspect of the distinctive Byzantine culture was its religion. Long before, Constantine had established the East's own separate branch of the church. This Eastern Church had leaders called patriarchs as counterparts to the popes, as the Rome-based religious heads were called. In time the Eastern Church would develop into several offshoots collectively known as the Orthodox Church.

The fate of the Byzantines was, for centuries, very unlike that of the former Western Roman Empire. Instead of turmoil, disorganization, and poverty, the Eastern Empire generally prospered during this period.

The Byzantine Empire's Fortunes Rise and Fall

This prosperity and the overall stability it created had several causes, notably its key location along trade routes connecting Europe to the Middle East, North Africa, and beyond. This gave the Byzantines the power to control commerce—and thus to accumulate tremendous wealth through taxes and other forms of income. But as all empires do, the Byzantine Empire eventually declined. The death of Justinian in 565 resulted in civil strife, which in turn left the empire vulnerable to a series of invasions by the Persians, Arabs, and Lombards among others. As a result of these invasions, the Byzantines suffered a devastating loss of territory.

The Byzantine Empire never fully recovered. Wickham comments, "The seriousness of these conquests for the Byzantine world cannot be overemphasized. . . . The empire lost two-thirds of its land and three-quarters of its wealth in the 610s . . . and this loss became permanent in the 630s."[24] Europe would not see anything that compared with the unified forces of the Frankish and Byzantine Empires until the middle of the tenth century, when a new entity, the Holy Roman Empire, emerged. In the meantime an increasingly strong power—the church—was influencing kingdoms all across Europe.

Chapter 3 🌐

The Power of the Church

Beginning with the Roman Empire, the fortunes of Europe's various realms intertwined with those of an increasingly powerful force: the Christian Church. Steadily, kings and leaders, including those of barbarian tribes, were converted to Christianity; they often persuaded or forced their subjects to do the same.

Christianity's importance on the European continent began to grow in 380, when Roman emperor Theodosius formally declared it his empire's official religion. The faith spread quickly after that. Chris Wickham notes, "Christian vocabulary, imagery, and public practice were thus politically dominant in the empire by the 400s, a dominance that would only increase thereafter; and in cities, which were the foci [centers] for almost all political activity, Christians were for the most part numerically dominant as well."[25]

Christianity Finds Acceptance

The close connection between religion and politics—between church and state, to use a modern phrase—is ancient and widespread. In the case of European Christianity, it began during the heyday of the Romans, as missionaries spread Christianity from its origin in the Middle East into the Mediterranean region and beyond. This process was by no means smooth; resistance to the new religion, within the empire and among the barbarian tribes outside it, was frequently passionate to the point of violence. Such violence led, in some cases, to incidences of martyrdom, when Roman leaders persecuted Christians—people who were so dedicated to their religion that they would rather die than deny that devotion. However, cases of extreme persecution grew increasingly rare over time. Many Roman subjects and members of barbarian tribes found the new religion appealing and its highly organized structure admirable. Increasingly, these tribes left their pagan (non-Christian) ways behind.

Christianity also found a major patron in Roman emperor Constantine, who ruled between 306 and 337. He officially banned the persecution of Christians and personally converted to the faith in 313. Constantine believed he had a moral obligation to spread his new religion throughout his realm. His example set a precedent that

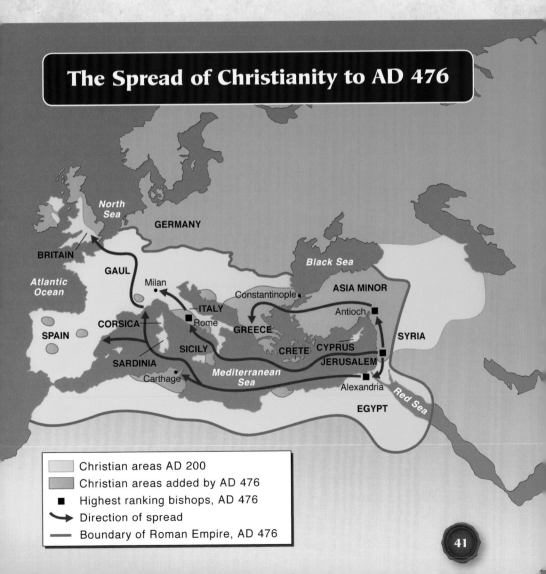

The Spread of Christianity to AD 476

- North Sea
- GERMANY
- BRITAIN
- GAUL
- Atlantic Ocean
- Milan
- Black Sea
- Constantinople
- ASIA MINOR
- ITALY
- Antioch
- Rome
- GREECE
- CORSICA
- SPAIN
- SICILY
- CRETE
- CYPRUS
- SYRIA
- SARDINIA
- JERUSALEM
- Carthage
- Mediterranean Sea
- Alexandria
- Red Sea
- EGYPT

Legend:
- Christian areas AD 200
- Christian areas added by AD 476
- ■ Highest ranking bishops, AD 476
- → Direction of spread
- — Boundary of Roman Empire, AD 476

his successors followed, and the tradition of spreading the religion through missionary work lasted for a thousand years.

At the head of the church was a single leader, called the pope. As the church steadily spread across Europe, the church—and by extension the pope—began to grow powerful, and it wielded increasing influence over both politics and everyday life. It affected large affairs; leaders who might otherwise have been enemies found a common bond in Christianity. And it affected small affairs as well; everyday people knew the hours of the day when they heard church bells toll. In such ways the church dominated the day-to-day lives of people from all walks of life, from royalty and nobility to tradespeople, artists, and workers in the fields.

A Unifying Religion

Sometimes the church and the kingdoms of Europe were closely allied. Indeed, at times they were virtually inseparable, such as when Charlemagne formed a political alliance with Pope Leo III. At other times the church came into deep conflict with the leader of a country or tribe. Sometimes their disagreements became so soured that two opposing kingdoms—one supported by the church, one not—went to war over religious matters, as when Charlemagne invaded Lombardy, at the request of Pope Adrian I, when the Lombards attempted to overthrow the papacy (office of the pope).

On the whole, however, the church significantly helped unify the continent. As more people converted to Christianity, and as more kingdoms were joined by their religion, the continent's geopolitical structure began to cohere. Christianity bound them together as a single entity under one faith.

This entity was Europe, although that name was not widely used until the end of the early Middle Ages. J.M. Roberts comments, "In the tenth century a few men had begun to apply the word 'Europe' to much of this zone; a Spanish chronicle had even spoken of the victors of [a war in] 732 as 'European.'"[26] This concept of the continent as a distinct geopolitical identity can be directly traced to the church's influence.

Donations to the Church

Lords in the early medieval era often gave generously to the church. They did this in large part to show their devotion, to increase their standing with clergy, and to make possible the forgiving of their sins and thus guarantee their place in heaven. One common act was to donate land, usually to a monastery near their homes. This excerpt is from a seventh-century document concerning such a grant.

> In the name of God, I have settled in my mind that I ought, for the good of my soul, to make a gift of something from my possessions, which I have therefore done. And this is what I hand over. . . . All those possessions of mine which there my father left me at his death [including] the courtyard with its buildings, with slaves, houses, lands cultivated and uncultivated, meadows, woods, waters, mills, etc.
>
> These . . . I hand over to the church, which was built in honor of *such and such a saint* to the monastery which is called *so and so*, where *such and such* an abbot is acknowledged to rule regularly over God's flock. [If] I myself or any other person shall wish to violate the firmness and validity of this grant, the order of truth opposing him, may his falsity in no degree succeed; and for his bold attempt may he pay to the aforesaid monastery double the amount which his ill-ordered cupidity [greed] has been prevented from abstracting; and moreover let him be culpable to the royal authority. . . . And, nevertheless, let the present charter remain inviolate with all that it contains, with the witnesses placed below.

Quoted in Dana Carlton Munro, ed., *Translations and Reprints from the Original Sources of European History*, Department of History of the University of Pennsylvania. www.shsu.edu.

Christendom

Significant portions of the Continent, such as the Scandinavian kingdoms, initially resisted conversion. However, Christianity soon dominated most portions of Europe, including about half of the Iberian Peninsula as well as much of modern-day France, Germany, Austria, and Italy. Colin McEvedy writes that this political domination by a combined religious and political force emphasized the ongoing fusion of religion and politics: "Church and State had fused to form a new society, Christendom."[27]

Charlemagne was not the first Christian Frankish king, but his strongly held beliefs and his desire to convert his subjects contributed to the rapid spread of Christianity in Europe.

This rapid spread was due in large part to Charlemagne's deep Christian beliefs and the obligation he felt to convert his empire to the faith. Frankish kings had been Christians for centuries, beginning with Clovis, the first of the Merovingian leaders. Legend has it that Clovis became the first Frankish king to convert. According to one historian of the time, this event occurred in the midst of war—on a battlefield in 496.

Faced with overwhelming odds and the prospect of certain defeat, Clovis prayed, saying, "Jesus Christ, if you will give me victory over my enemies, I will believe in you. I have called upon my own gods, but, as I see only too clearly, they have no intention of helping me."[28] Legend has it that shortly after this, the enemy unexpectedly broke ranks and surrendered. Clovis was convinced.

Monasticism

Both before and after Clovis's conversion, one of the most important elements of the church's structure—in terms of spreading the faith, and of Christian society as a whole—was the monastic tradition. Monasticism refers to the practice, which still exists, of monks and nuns, their female counterparts, who retreat from the everyday world and gave themselves to a life of devotion and prayer.

Monks and nuns generally led very strict lives. They were celibate and typically lived in secluded communities called monasteries and convents. Particular orders often had additional restrictions, such as silence or poverty. (To a lesser degree, this is all still the case.) Some religious orders then (as now) were not entirely secluded, however. They took on such tasks as caring for the sick or providing travelers with accommodations.

The Christian monastic tradition did not begin in the Middle Ages; some very early Christians had long before lived lives of solitude and religious reflection, mostly in the deserts of the Holy Land. However, as Christianity spread, so did monasticism, and it reached new heights of refinement during medieval times. By the sixth century, monasticism was a common aspect of life in western Europe.

A Life Devoted to Religious Faith

Many people were drawn to the isolated, contemplative life of a monk or nun. This was true for some peasants; a life spent in a monastery or convent was attractive when the alternative was an existence of back-breaking, unrelieved labor. But it was also true for significant numbers within the nobility, who thought of a life devoted to religious faith as an honorable path.

It appealed particularly to men and women of the higher classes who were educated, intelligent, and strong in character. As a result, monks became the backbone of the maintenance and development of such subjects as science, mathematics, astronomy, medicine, languages, and philosophy during this period. The monastic tradition thus played a significant role in shaping the civilization of the Middle Ages.

Some monks devoted themselves to educating young people in the schools that they operated. Of course, this helped the spread of learning. However, despite the relative rise in education and literacy, church officials often remained the only people in a given district who could read and write. In part this was because they wanted to retain their usual role as the primary—and, in some cases, only—people who could read the Bible. (At this point in history, the Bible was available only in Latin.) This, by extension, let them continue the Christian tradition that only priests could perform masses and have direct communication with God.

The ability to read had more advantages as well for church officials. It gave them considerable power in society and government, because they were often called on to serve royalty and nobility with their literacy. The clergy could read and write down laws; they also had the ability to compose letters, messages from one region to another, and other important documents. In turn, this gave them opportunities to influence political matters.

The monastic life was, overall, a serious one. However, if some accounts are to be believed, some monks and nuns strayed. They were accused—and apparently guilty—of enjoying the secular (nonreligious) life too much, indulging in such scandalous pleasures as taking lovers or enjoying an excess of wine and food. McEvedy comments that

Pope Gregory I

Pope Gregory I, who lived from about 540 to 604, was a very important figure in medieval religious history. Many of his actions had significant and lasting repercussions for the church. Among other things, Gregory was responsible for reforming the Mass (including the development of Gregorian chant, a way of combining music with the Mass). He also was instrumental in defining the role of priests and monks, founding monasteries, and helping the sick and poor. Furthermore, Gregory I did much to strengthen the power of the papacy, notably by greatly increasing the church's land holdings across Europe and North Africa and by gaining governmental and political control of much of the Italian Peninsula (a control that lasted for centuries).

Gregory also extended and amplified the understanding that the papacy was the church's supreme and decisive authority—an understanding that has existed to this day. Furthermore, he worked to create a long-sought goal for the papacy: a close bond between church and state. All of this earned him the title "the Great" after his name—making him one of three popes to be so honored.

monks sometimes got into trouble with their superiors—both religious and royal—because they "rollicked too loud and too often."[29]

The Rule of Benedict

To curb this trend, a code of conduct was written in the sixth century by Benedict (later St. Benedict), an Italian monk and the founder of the Benedictine order of monks. Over the course of about a decade, the monk wrote a manifesto later called the *Rule of Saint Benedict*, which laid down details of proper conduct for his fellow monks. These principles spread quickly across Europe and were accepted as a standard. They were then added to and modified by some of the many different monastic orders that developed in later centuries.

Some of Benedict's rules ensured a high degree of separation from the rest of the world and an existence composed mainly of prayer and work. On the other hand, Benedict was less strict about some things. For example, he stated his belief that monks should be given healthy and sufficient food, a moderate amount of wine, and enough sleep. He was not interested in the denial of basic sustenance, which some monks advocated as a means of purification.

Furthermore, Benedict wrote of his belief that monks had an obligation to help those less fortunate. He outlined that this could be fulfilled in such ways as helping the poor, visiting the sick, and burying the dead. He stated, "We desire to dwell in the tabernacle of God's kingdom, and if we fulfill the duties of tenants [of that building], we shall be heirs of the kingdom of heaven."[30]

Charlemagne's Influence

By the 800s, monasticism—and Christianity overall—was more a part of daily life in Europe than ever before. This was especially true in the Frankish Empire, where Charlemagne's rule was at its apex. Charlemagne was not the first European ruler to become a Christian and was not even the first in his own dynasty. However, he proved to be the most influential, doing everything in his power to support his faith.

Charlemagne saw himself as a successor to the later Roman emperors, so it was natural that he wanted to make Christianity the official religion of his realm, as they had done before him. Furthermore, he set an example for his subjects through his strong support of religious culture. Roberts notes, "What was . . . striking was the seriousness with which he took his Christian role and the promotion of [religious] learning and art; he wanted to magnify his kingship by filling his court with evidence of Christian culture."[31]

As might be expected, Charlemagne insisted that all of his subjects should be Christian as well—even if this had to be done by force. For example, when a 30-year war with the Saxons ended in 804 as a victory for Charlemagne, the vanquished tribe was forced to accept certain religious conditions. Einhard, Charlemagne's biographer, stated that in addition to requiring "union with the Franks to form one people," the ruler insisted on "renunciation of their national religious customs and the worship of devils [and] acceptance of the sacraments of the Christian faith and religion."[32]

Charlemagne and Pope Leo III

The price of disobedience on this issue was steep. If individuals or groups refused Charlemagne's orders to convert or secretly defied them, the result was usually brutality and bloodshed. According to legend, for instance, at one point Charlemagne ordered the beheading of some 4,500 Saxons who had ostensibly become Christians, but who had been caught practicing their native paganism in secret.

But Charlemagne's mission was not always conducted through violence. He also boosted Christianity's cause—and his—through diplomatic means. This primarily happened by maintaining a close relationship with the papacy. The most significant outcome of these ties between the Frankish king and church leaders concerned Pope Leo III. After the pope was elected in 795, the two formed a close bond. This was cemented when the new pope soon found himself in serious danger.

From Frankish King to Emperor

Leo came from humble stock, and his election to his new office infuriated the upper classes of Roman society. One of his rivals plotted against Leo, and in 799 the pope was attacked while taking part in a procession through the city to celebrate a religious holiday. His attackers' intent was apparently not to kill Leo, but to render him unfit to continue as

In the year 800, Pope Leo III crowned Charlemagne emperor, as depicted in this page from a fourteenth-century illuminated manuscript (opposite). The emperor ruled over all Christian lands, an area that essentially included all of western Europe.

pope. To this end they tried to blind him and tear his tongue out, and they left him bleeding in the street. In any case Leo survived the attack and was taken to a monastery in the north. (According to one legend his eyes and tongue miraculously healed.)

Leo then continued north into Charlemagne's domain, where the Frankish king warmly welcomed him. After some months there, the recovered pope returned to Rome under the protection of Charlemagne's men. In the following year, 800, the king joined him there.

Leo, of course, was deeply grateful to the king. He showed this affection in a dramatic way: On Christmas Day of 800, in a lavish and solemn ceremony, he crowned the ruler *Imperator Romanorum* (Roman emperor). This was a position of tremendous prestige and power; Charlemagne now officially ruled over all Christian lands—essentially all of western Europe, not just his own realm.

Charlemagne always insisted that this honor came as a surprise. Some experts are skeptical of this, though others give it credence. Geoffrey Barraclough, one of the latter, comments, "If one thing is certain, it is that the initiative for the imperial coronation did not come from Charles' [Charlemagne's] side."[33]

A Failure to Merge Empires

Whether or not he was surprised, the ruler accepted the title. Leo, meanwhile, had more on his mind than simply showing his gratitude. The pope hoped that aligning himself with the politically and militarily powerful Charlemagne would increase his own power and prestige. One immediate advantage for Leo was that he could assert that only the pope had the right to crown an imperial ruler and, further, that he and all future popes were superior to the emperor.

Leo also saw the occasion of the coronation as a chance to assert dominance over the Byzantine Empire, which had never fully recovered from the loss of much of its land in the mid-600s to Muslim forces. Adding to Leo's belief that he could dominate Byzantium was the fact that a woman, Empress Irene of Greece, was now the Byzantine ruler. The pope perceived her as weak and vulnerable. A Frankish cleric of the time noted, "When, in the land of the Greeks, there was no longer an emperor and when the imperial power was being exercised by a woman, it seemed to Pope Leo himself and . . . to the whole Christian people that it would be fitting to give the title of [Roman emperor] to the king of the Franks, Charles."[34]

Leo hoped that crowning Charlemagne as the powerful new Roman emperor would be another step toward controlling the Byzantine Empire. Henri Pirenne, a distinguished historian, comments, "Because the Byzantines had proved so unsatisfactory from every point of view—political, military and doctrinal—he [the pope] would select a westerner: the one man who by his wisdom and statesmanship and the vastness of his dominions . . . stood out head and shoulders above his contemporaries."[35]

One of the steps Leo and Charlemagne took was to suggest an arranged marriage between the newly crowned emperor and Irene. According to some sources, she considered it seriously but eventually declined. The marriage might have ended the long-standing differences between the empires. After it failed to transpire, however, the cultural and political gap only grew larger. Charlemagne's death in 814, and the resulting loss of Frankish military power, more or less put an end to any possibility that the rift between East and West might be healed.

Otto the Great

The next significant turning point for the church, in terms of its role in the political life of the early Middle Ages, took place in the century after the death of Charlemagne, when another pope and another powerful ruler forged a lasting alliance. The wheels for this were set in motion in 936, with the death of Henry the Fowler, the Germanic king of East Francia and a descendant of Charlemagne. Henry's throne went to his son, Otto (also called Otto the Great), an ambitious ruler who aggressively expanded his territory. One of his major military victories was the defeat of the Magyars, who originally came from what is now Hungary but occupied huge regions of central Europe by the 900s. Otto's defeat of this tribe gave him control over their land and its valuable deposits of lead, copper, and silver. The wealth that these resources brought Otto enabled him to further his empire-building plans.

From the beginning of his reign, Otto had explicitly seen himself as the successor to the mighty Charlemagne. One of the cornerstones of Charlemagne's reign had been his close relationship with the church, and Otto emulated this in several ways. For example, he began a policy of placing elite members of the clergy in positions of power. He gave clerics important administrative positions, often favoring them over nonclerical nobles who would traditionally have been granted the posts. As Charlemagne had done, Otto was thus able to link political power with the authority of an influential religious body. McEvedy comments that under Otto's rule, "Church and state acted as one."[36]

Otto Becomes Emperor

The bond between Otto and the church became even closer as the result of political turmoil in Italy in the early 960s, specifically involving Adelaide, the queen of Italy. As a young woman, Adelaide was caught up in a deadly political plot: As the daughter, daughter-in-law, and widow of the last three kings of Italy, she inherited that country's throne. But a rival nobleman, Berengar II of Ivrea, kidnapped Adelaide in 951, imprisoned her, and declared himself king. (He may also have poisoned Adelaide's husband.) Berengar tried to force Adelaide to marry his son, which would have legitimized his family's claim over the Italian kingdom.

After several months, however, Adelaide managed to escape. According to legend she did this by digging a tunnel, aided by a sympathetic priest, under the walls of the castle where she was held prisoner. Adelaide sent a messenger north to Otto, asking him to intervene on her behalf. He responded immediately, sending an army across the Alps, taking her away from danger—and then marrying her.

This was a shrewd move for both Otto and Adelaide. It merged the kingdom of Italy (today's northern Italy) to the land Otto already possessed, which comprised, in part, West and East Francia. It also furthered Otto's plan to forge a close relationship with one of Adelaide's political supporters: John XII, the influential but scandalous pope then in office. Early in 962 John crowned Otto emperor. In return Otto promised to recognize John as the legitimate pope despite serious accusations of corruption, adultery, and murder.

However, the alliance between the pope and the new emperor soon soured. John, growing wary of Otto's increasing power, plotted with Byzantine rulers to overthrow him. But Otto was able to move more quickly, and he assembled a group of sympathetic church bishops who planned to replace John.

Open war between supporters of both sides threatened to erupt, but John died before this could happen. He was replaced by Benedict V, but only briefly; after one month Otto forced Benedict out and arranged the installation of his choice, Leo VIII. Following this event, Otto declared that no pope could be elected without explicit approval of the emperor. This marked a significant shift in the balance of power between religion and government, foreshadowing what became, in the next centuries, the church's slowly waning political clout.

The Holy Roman Empire

In time the lands that Otto controlled would be known as the Holy Roman Empire, and Otto would be considered its first leader. This empire—which, despite its name, did not include Rome for most of its history—would reach a peak in the following centuries, encompassing the kingdoms of Germany, Italy, and Burgundy, along with hundreds of smaller principalities, duchies, counties, cities, and other domains.

Otto the Great—and before him, Charlemagne and other rulers—brought to a new peak the complex, sometimes close and sometimes warring relationships between the dominant religion and the dominant states of the Middle Ages. All in all, the influence of the church was a tremendously powerful force in the development of Europe's geographic and political structures.

Chapter 4

The Rise of Feudalism

I n addition to the church, another social element permeated the lives of everyone, from highborn to lowborn, during the early Middle Ages. This was a complex system called feudalism. A somewhat similar social structure had existed before then, in ancient Rome; a much more highly codified system began to take shape under Clovis and matured during Charlemagne's reign.

"The Keynote of Society"

For centuries after Charlemagne's rule, feudalism continued to play a major role in virtually every facet of society and economics, determining everything from relationships between kings and lords to how farmers grew and made use of their crops. It also had a dramatic effect on the military, judicial, legislative, and administrative aspects of society.

Simply put, feudalism was an arrangement among people in different social classes. The socially higher person offered protection, patronage, and some kind of reward, usually in the form of profit from some kind of activity. In exchange the person in the lower social stratum promised loyalty, to serve in some capacity, and to deliver profit of some kind, such as crops or a portion of money earned. Historian Marjorie Rowling writes, "In a period when wars and famine were incessant, service, in exchange for protection, became the keynote of society."[37]

Feudalism was strongest among Europe's rural cultures, which existed during the early Middle Ages mainly in France, Germany, England,

Peasants work the land surrounding the castle, as depicted in this fifteenth-century painting. As both laborers and tenant farmers, peasants played an essential role in the land-based feudal system that began developing during the early Middle Ages.

and other northern European countries. The more urban regions along the Mediterranean, such as Italy, Spain, and southern France, never fully adopted the system. In part this was because urban life depended less heavily on the feudal system than rural life.

The Agricultural Base

The primary driving force behind feudalism was economics. Europe in the Middle Ages was overwhelmingly rural, so for all practical purposes economics meant agriculture. Feudalism was directly tied to land: how it was used and who received the benefits from working it.

In an agricultural world, land equals wealth: The more in one's possession, the richer one is. If a harvest is good, the economy is generally stable and robust; if not, the result is poverty and starvation. During the early Middle Ages, economist Kenneth Jupp comments, "land paid virtually all the costs of government . . . throughout most of Europe."[38]

A crucial point, therefore, was who owned and managed the land. The Romans had believed in private ownership of land. Barbarian tribes, meanwhile, typically shared it communally. Under feudalism, however, the king owned all the land; below him were lords (also called nobles) who were awarded parcels of land of various sizes. Within these parcels were manors, similar to large farming tracts, awarded to knights—elite soldiers in the lords' employ—or to lesser lords, all of whom were typically allowed to keep the profits from the land. Below them were peasants, the laborers who worked the manor's land.

Fiefs

The parcels of land awarded by the king, typically given for service in battle or in other ways, were called fiefs. Profit from this land, besides crops, came from grazing and fishing rights, forest products such as timber, and animals, including livestock and game. Sometimes a fief was not land but something else that created income, such as a mill or a license to collect taxes in a certain area.

Dividing a Kingdom

A king owned all of the land within his realm and had absolute power to do with it as he pleased. Sometimes this meant awarding parcels of land to loyal nobles. Sometimes, however, it meant directly passing it on to his royal successors. This passage is from Charlemagne's *Divisio Regnorum*, the king's official declaration of how he planned to divide his lands between his three sons:

> So as not to leave my sons a confused and unsettled matter of dispute and contention as regards the status of my entire kingdom, I have divided the whole body of the realm into three portions; the portion that each of them is to guard and rule, I have caused to be described and designated. I have done this so that each may be content with his portion in accord with my ruling. And so that each may strive to defend the borders of his kingdom which face foreign peoples and maintain peace and charity with his brothers.

Quoted in "Louis the Pious: A Brief Overview of the Changing French Landscape, 806–843," Louis the Pious: History and Maps, Eckerd College Community. http://home.eckerd.edu.

Fief holders truly needed the income from these sources. For one thing, they had grand manor houses and castles that had to be kept up, with all of the maintenance and labor expenses that entailed. For another, they had enormous expenses connected to the upkeep of knights, horses, and soldiers.

Typically, the rights to operate a fief and to hold titles were hereditary—that is, passed down from one generation to the next, usually through the male line. If a lord had no heir, the land often was passed on to the church as a sign of piety. Monasteries were major landholders all across Europe, and were thus important employers. Furthermore, monasteries frequently acted on behalf of absentee owners, especially in newly conquered lands far away. In this way, as in so many other aspects of medieval life, the church played an important role in the feudal system.

The Life of a Lord

Generally speaking, lords were the absolute authority within their fiefdoms. They administered justice, gathered taxes, and managed how crops were grown. They could even decide if and with whom their subjects could marry.

The management of a fief took a lot of time. It was generally considered beneath a lord's dignity to do any farmwork himself—he was a manager. His wife, meanwhile, would be expected to do the same in the house, managing a large staff of servants and making sure things ran smoothly. Their sons (and sometimes daughters) typically were educated by private tutors or in nearby religious schools.

Unlike the workers under them, lords had the leisure to indulge in many other activities. Prayer, of course, was one important activity, but there were many other things that could be excellent pastimes. One writer of the time, in a book about proper noble behavior, noted that a member of that class "should lead a life in keeping with his status, exercising himself with hunting and enjoying those things which others provide him with their labors."[39]

The Life of a Knight

Hunting was perhaps the most common outdoor pastime for knights, usually with bow and arrows. A knight could spend hours or even days on expeditions by horseback, wielding his weapons and directing a group through woods and over open ground. Hunting groups typically included friends, household members, and visitors, plus a large number of dog handlers and other servants.

French knights on horseback give spectators a taste of the battlefield during a tournament. Contests between knights could be savage and deadly.

Tournaments were also popular outdoor activities. These were mock battles that were very popular in times of peace for warriors who missed the excitement of battle. For these mock combats, groups of knights gathered to fight each other in teams. Knights used real weapons in tournaments, and the clashes, which lasted for several days, could be savage and even deadly. Winners received prizes, and captured knights were held for small, but real, ransoms.

In the early days of the Middle Ages, the church and some kings disapproved of tournaments. They considered the contests bloody, wasteful, and undignified. Henry II of England banned them completely. Eventually, however, tournaments gained popularity even with royalty. Tournaments became so popular that many knights traveled from contest to contest, like modern-day rodeo cowboys, since an outstanding knight could make a good living with them.

Peasants and Serfs

The laborers who worked the fields of a fiefdom, as might be expected, did not have the time for much luxury. These workers were called peasants. Sometimes their superiors directly employed them. Sometimes, however, peasants were allowed to be tenant farmers, a more complicated arrangement in which peasants leased the use of farmland from their lords.

Peasants had hard lives and not many privileges, but they were still not the lowest class in the medieval social ladder. An even lower order was that of menial workers called serfs. Although serfs were free, in many ways they were close to being slaves. They were bound so tightly to their manors by oaths of loyalty that they were essentially trapped; in theory they could leave, but in practical terms this was not likely. If they quit, they would not only lose their jobs but also their safety, since they would have no protection from bandits, rogue knights, greedy lords, or other enemies.

Being a peasant or a serf was typically hereditary. Often, if a manor passed out of the hands of a lord, the serfs associated with it stayed and served their new lord. Meanwhile, outright slavery, a holdover from ancient Roman times, was still practiced in some parts of Europe, especially in the south. Historians estimate that slaves constituted 10 to 20 percent of the rural population of Europe during the early Middle Ages.

Fealty

The feudal system was largely driven by economics, but it encompassed more than land ownership and management. Feudalism was also a complex social arrangement that defined relationships among the separate social classes. Typically, these relationships were based on personal ties; for example, a lord might guarantee a peasant a place on his land because the peasant's family had worked there for generations. Such personal connections were crucial—perhaps more so than any legal agreements could have been. J.M. Roberts notes,

"Even where 'feudal' tenures [the holding of land or a guarantee of work] might exist, considerations of honour and status often counted for more in shaping behaviour."[40]

The essential aspect of these arrangements was loyalty. A member of a given class swore loyalty to the person above him, making a solemn promise called an oath of fealty. This connection proceeded up and down the entire feudal order.

The High Cost of Fealty

When a king gave a lord a fief, or that lord gave part of it to a lesser noble, the one receiving the gift swore to be his superior's man. Knights, for instance, promised to answer a call to war, fighting for their lords a certain number of days out of each year—and to the death, if necessary.

Fealty was sworn in a special ceremony. Such ceremonies were important, in large part because contracts were rarely written down during this period—and not many could have read a contract even if it existed. Having a ceremony to mark the occasion was thus an important part of the pledge of fealty. Another typical symbol of fealty to a lord was the wearing of special livery—that is, clothing that clearly identified a person as part of his superior's domain.

Peasants, who worked the fields and served their lords in other ways, were entitled to only a portion of a fief's profits—typically just enough to feed their families. Most of it went to the lord who managed the land, and a significant portion made its way up the chain to the king, typically in the form of an annual tax—a "gift" called a tribute. Tributes were also symbols of loyalty in addition to their obvious purpose of financial profit. And sometimes a lord was expected to demonstrate his fealty to his king by providing for him when the monarch traveled through his land.

Clearly, such an obligation could have serious costs. One example recorded a Christmastime visit to a lord, late in the eleventh century, by William the Conqueror, the king of England. In just a few days of feasting, the king and his entourage consumed 6,000 chickens, 1,000

Under feudalism, people swore oaths of loyalty to the lords from whom they received land and protection. This is a typical oath from the seventh century.

> Since it is known familiarly to all how little I have whence to feed and clothe myself, I have therefore petitioned your piety, and your good-will has decreed to me that I should hand myself over or commend myself to your guardianship, which I have thereupon done; that is to say in this way, that you should aid and succor me as well with food as with clothing, according as I shall be able to serve you and deserve it.
>
> And so long as I shall live I ought to provide service and honor to you, suitably to my free condition; and I shall not during the time of my life have the ability to withdraw from your power or guardianship; but must remain during the days of my life under your power or defense. Wherefore it is proper that if either of us shall wish to withdraw himself from these agreements, he shall pay [a fee] to the other party . . . and this agreement shall remain unbroken.

Quoted in Dana Carlton Munro, *A History of the Middle Ages*. Ithaca, NY: Cornell University Press, 2009, p. 41.

rabbits, 90 boars, 50 peacocks, 200 geese, 10,000 eels, thousands of eggs and loaves of bread, and hundreds of casks of wine and cider. Chris Wickham wryly comments, "Loyalty cost more than a few cups of wine."[41]

A Chain with Many Links

In return for their pledges of fealty, lords received the promise of protection from enemies and support in time of trouble. They also received prestigious and influential positions of authority, such as regional administrative posts. This administrative arrangement allowed a ruler to sustain a large realm without having to deal with day-to-day problems in individual provinces.

In this way vassals (a general term for someone who swore loyalty to a higher master) were part of the string of mutual aid that ran from the top of society to the bottom and back. Roberts notes, "As the relationships elaborated, vassals came to have their own vassals and one lord's man might be another man's lord. A chain of obligation could stretch (in theory) from the king down through his great men and their retainers to the lowest of the free."[42]

Some experts argue that feudalism was not entirely unfair in its division of social classes. They point out that, in some ways, these classes had a degree of equality, because everyone had responsibilities to others. Jupp comments, "It was indeed a system of unequal hereditary status. Yet it stood for a kind of justice, because no one was so high that his privileges were not conditional upon the discharge of obligations, and no one was so low that he was without certain rights."[43]

The Manor House and Its Surroundings

As might be expected, feudalism had a dramatic effect on how people in the medieval era lived their daily lives. For one thing, the system affected the physical layout of manors and the lands and villages surrounding them.

Typically, the manor house—the home of the local noble family—was the grandest structure around, except for the church. Manor houses were typically two or three stories high and built of wood and stone. A typical manor house featured a huge entry/receiving hall, a private chapel, multiple bedrooms and other chambers, a kitchen and pantry, and other rooms. Wall tapestries and huge fireplaces provided warmth.

Surrounding the manor house were farm buildings, such as horse stables and structures for grain storage. Peasants typically lived in nearby huts with dirt floors and thatched roofs made of thick layers of straw or hay. Farther away would be a village or two, woods, and fields. A medium-sized estate might encompass 400 to 600 acres (162 to 243 ha) in total. Peter S. Wells comments, "The contrast between the small wattle-and-daub huts in which most people lived and the great stone, plaster, and tile houses of the wealthy, with their painted walls and decorative mosaics, indicates the differences between groups within early European societies."[44]

A typical fief needed several dozen peasant families to maintain it, grow crops, and raise livestock. In contrast to the lives of lords and their families, the life of a peasant mostly consisted of hard, monotonous work: planting and harvesting, raising and slaughtering livestock. However, even considering that most of what a fief produced was not theirs to keep, peasants could still generally get by.

This was especially so if they were tenant farmers. In a good year a family of tenant farmers could make a comfortable living working about 30 acres (12ha) and raising a few animals. Peasants might also be allowed to hunt with bow and arrows as a means of supplementing their income, although a lord had the right to forbid this.

Light Without Brightness

Of course, many factors could disrupt the lives of everyone from the lowliest serfs to privileged aristocrats. For one thing, the primitive level of medicine at the time, combined with other factors, meant that the average life span for a person in the early Middle Ages was only about 33 years.

Another devastating factor was famine. Since transportation was limited to foot, boat, or wagon traffic, perishable food could travel only short distances. People ate only local food, and a single bad harvest could cause serious shortages. One prominent example of this was a serious freeze in the winter of 535–536 that caused widespread crop failures and livestock deaths—and thus human deaths—across the continent (and the rest of the world as well).

Several sources from the time speak of this event, the best known being the Byzantine historian Procopius, who wrote, "During this year a most dread portent [omen] took place. For the sun gave forth its light without brightness . . . and it seemed exceedingly like the sun in eclipse, for the beams it shed were not clear."[45] According to one story Scandinavian kings sacrificed a fortune in gold to their gods, hoping the warmth would return.

The Plague

An even greater calamity than famine—one that also had no respect for social standing—was disease. Typhus, influenza, and smallpox were only three of the most serious diseases that swept through Europe, killing thousands, during the early medieval period. (The spread of disease was greatly aided by common beliefs of the time regarding sanitation. For example, most people believed that bathing was dangerous to the health, and it was not uncommon for someone to bathe only once a year.)

One of the worst of the deadly epidemics to sweep Europe was the Plague of Justinian, which had overwhelmed the Byzantine Empire in 541–542, during that emperor's reign. This epidemic, the first clearly recorded incidence of bubonic plague, might have originated in Ethiopia or Egypt and might have spread via grain ships that supplied massive amounts of grain to the city of Constantinople to feed its citizens. Rats, and the fleas that live on them, are carriers of the plague, which is easily transferred to humans. The grain ships thus were likely the source of contagion for the city, and the massive public granaries of the vast city only served to nurture its rat and flea population.

The plague was swift and horrifying in its destructive power. It caused painful swellings, followed by unbearable fever and death within days or even hours. This was only the effect on individuals; the disease was epic in its overall destruction as well. At its peak, according to one record of the time, the plague killed 10,000 people every day in Constantinople alone, although this figure may be inflated. The city quickly ran out of land to use as burial sites, and bodies were left in stacks out in the open. By the time the scourge ended, an estimated 40 percent of the city's inhabitants were dead. Nor was the epidemic confined to Constantinople; it has been estimated that it caused the deaths of as many as 100 million people as it rapidly spread across the eastern Mediterranean and into central Europe.

The Byzantine Empire Succumbs to the Plague

The Plague of Justinian did not only have sweeping consequences in terms of the loss of human life. It also had a significant impact on the Byzantine Empire's economics. Justinian I was in great need of tax money, notably because of vast expenditures on wars against barbarians in what is now Italy. He had also pledged major funds for the construction of great churches, like Constantinople's magnificent Hagia Sophia cathedral. The plague had a disastrous effect on his ability to collect taxes, since the number of people in his empire who could either pay them or administer them had dropped so dramatically.

Meanwhile, the devastation gave outside invaders better opportunities to attack. The plague thus weakened the Byzantine Empire at a critical point in its history, just as Justinian's armies were on the verge of retaking land in Italy and the western Mediterranean coast. But Justinian's overextended troops could not hold on. Even after the plague subsided, they could not move farther afield than Italy. The empire quickly lost nearly all of its territory, and Justinian's death was followed by centuries of war with barbarian tribes.

A World of Haves and Have-Nots

Plagues continued to sweep the continent throughout the early Middle Ages, at the rate of roughly one per generation. It is estimated that half of the entire population of Europe died between 541 and 700 from outbreaks of disease. After 700, however, for unclear reasons, there were no more major outbreaks until the fourteenth century.

Clearly, life was hard during the feudal period. Disease and famine were major reasons why this was so. Another reason concerned the tight bonds of the feudal system. While in some ways beneficial, feudalism had the effect of dividing social classes into haves and have-nots. The have-nots, of course, had the hardest lives of all.

Chapter 5

What Is the Legacy of the Early Middle Ages?

The early Middle Ages planted the seeds of significant change in Europe. This was true for almost every part of life, including politics, religion, economics, and social structures. Many of the ideas and practices that became part of daily life during the early medieval era continued to influence life in the latter part of the Middle Ages and beyond. For example, the medieval economy, based on trading, barter, and the use of coinage, established rules for future commerce. Furthermore, the empires of Charlemagne and other medieval rulers laid the basis for the geopolitical structures that today define Europe. History professor Richard Hooker comments, "The model [Charlemagne] formed, a centralized government that consisted largely of independent local rulers, would become the foundation of the later innovations in government structure in the later Middle Ages."[46]

The Seeds of Representative Government

Another important legacy that had its roots in the early Middle Ages is the modern version of civil rights. During the earliest medieval centuries, the ruler of a given kingdom had absolute power over virtually everything. However, the seeds of a radical shift away from this single source of power were planted toward the end of this period. The shift would not genuinely blossom until later, but its beginnings can none-theless be seen during the early Middle Ages.

To a large degree, this shift involved an emerging ruling class, the aristocracy, rather than an absolute monarch. A variety of reasons lay behind this change, including the need to maintain control of increas-ingly larger areas as centralized empires took the place of small king-doms. Rulers needed to delegate power and governmental control to lords and knights.

These members of the upper classes were well suited to the task. They formed the basis for the political structure to come, which would see the emergence of more democratic forms of government (involv-ing representatives elected by citizens). In the meantime the lords and warriors of the aristocracy had trained all their lives to be in positions of leadership. They also displayed many of the hallmarks of modern politics: the ability to create consensus among diverse parties, seriously consider the opinions of others, and organize collective action. Further-more, they began to assert what they felt was an important obligation: to serve the people as a whole. Sociologist Gianfranco Poggi writes, "To this class [of lords and knights] feudalism attributed powers that went beyond those of a purely military nature, and in the exercise of which these warriors slowly but progressively learned to consider criteria of equity, to respect local traditions, to protect the weak, and to practice responsibility."[47]

As such attitudes became increasingly prominent, another crucial aspect of modern civilization emerged: the right of a citizen to deter-mine his or her own course. This was true, at least at first, only for the aristocracy. Nobles no longer felt the need to follow their rulers unthinkingly. Put simply, they felt justified in pushing back when their kings pushed them. For example, in 1022, a French count named Eudes composed a letter to King Robert II of France. In it he defended his decision not to attend a court case in which the king was due to render a judgment on the count. Eudes wrote: "You well know how I have served you in peace, in war, and on your travels, as long as you held me in your favor. But once you withdrew that favor from me . . . if I did anything that you found offensive while defending myself and my honor, I was pushed into it by the wrong done me and under the pressure of necessity."[48]

The Legacy of Urban Life

The development of cities and vibrant urban cultures has some roots in the early medieval era as well. Of course, cities had existed for several thousand years in some parts of the world. In early medieval Europe, however, most towns held only a few thousand people. Even large cities were, by today's standards, small, loosely organized, and haphazardly built.

Some urban centers, such as market towns, had distinctive identities, and life there had an individual flavor. Historian E.L. Knox notes that this was true even though rural people who moved there brought with them much of the flavor of country life. He writes, "There were many manifestations of rural life in the city: gardens, herds of livestock, even farms within the city walls. Yet townsmen saw themselves as distinct from country folk."[49]

The size and diverse nature of urban life intensified as more people moved from the countryside. As this happened, aspects of urban life—quite distinct from rural life—began to take shape. For example, urban social characteristics that today most city dwellers take for granted, such as anonymity and the possibility of self-invention, began to emerge. In other words the city made it possible for an ordinary person to create a new life with a high degree of freedom. Neighbors did not necessarily know everything (as would typically happen in a rural environment or small town), and people were no longer trapped in a single class or occupation, as was common under feudalism.

The Rise of Communes

The increase of people opting for an urban life also led to the early stages of several important social organizations and institutions, leaving a legacy that would flourish in centuries to come. Among the most prominent examples of these were associations called city communes.

At the foot of a hilltop castle, busy farmers and townspeople go about their daily activities, as depicted in this fifteenth-century drawing. The early medieval era contributed to the development of cities and vibrant urban cultures.

Communes were originally formed as loose organizations providing residents of a city with mutual support for protection against raiders—and occasionally against other problems, such as excessive taxation imposed by corrupt nobles. Communes also formed a buffer to the sharp divisions of class. Medieval scholar William W. Kibler writes, "Communes engaged all inhabitants in a communal oath [of solidarity], thus substituting a horizontal and egalitarian [equal] form of association for the more hierarchical [up and down] ones of the aristocracy."[50]

This informal banding together for protection soon became more formalized to include councils that governed and operated towns and cities. Although they still were subjects of their king, the members of a

The Size of Cities

Nearly every city in Europe in the early medieval period was small by today's standards. By the year 1000, there were still no large cities on most of the continent. The great seaports of Italy were the most populous city-states (city-states operated as independent countries) in the West, primarily because of their lucrative trade business with Constantinople and Alexandria in the East. For example, the northern Italian seaport city of Genoa had an estimated 80,000 inhabitants. Historian J.M. Roberts comments, "Such [European] towns as survived were mainly to be found in Italy, where commercial relations with the outside world had been sporadically kept up even amid the upheavals of first barbarian and then Arab invasions."

Things were different in the Byzantine Empire, however, since that realm enjoyed even greater prosperity through trade. Constantinople, for instance, had an estimated 300,000 to 500,000 people at its peak during the reign of Justinian.

J.M. Roberts, *A History of Europe*. New York: Allen Lane/Penguin, 1996, p. 131.

given commune had the power to govern themselves in ways that were more or less independent of outside influence.

The first commune may have been in Forlì, a city in northern Italy. Forlì established itself as an independent commune in about the year 889. The concept proved enormously popular, since it gave so many people a strong degree of control over their lives, and in the following centuries it spread to towns and cities across Europe. Some descendants of these medieval communes still exist, such as those in Italy that act cooperatively in the production of wine.

Guilds

A related element of urban life that began to develop during the early Middle Ages—one that can still be seen today in altered form—was the rise of guilds. Guilds were organizations made up of craftspeople or businesspeople. By the later part of the Middle Ages, there were guilds for virtually every trade or craft, such as cobblers, woodworkers, stonecutters, brewers, and bakers. Merchant guilds, meanwhile, were organized for such trades as dealers in produce or cloth.

Like members of today's labor unions, workers paid annual dues to belong to a guild. In return the guilds provided a number of services for their members. For example, a guild promised to support the family of sick or injured members and to arrange for members' burials.

A guild also promised protection, for property as well as people, when a member traveled outside the city walls. Guilds furthermore gave support to new business ventures or provided mediation in disputed cases. Members of guilds also pledged to defend each other from danger or unfair business practices, both from within and without the city walls, and to exact revenge or compensation if one member was attacked outside the town.

Business and Social Bonds

A number of rules governed how guild members operated. Typical rules included fair treatment of apprentices, young people who were learning a trade by working for an established craftsperson; the enforcement of bans or fines for those who were not guild members (essentially creating what today would be called a closed shop, in which only union members are hired); agreements on fair prices for goods and services; and quality standards—such as the use of marks such as patterns in loaves of bread. These marks guaranteed that a given product had been made under the auspices of a guild and thus was of guaranteed quality. They also served as a crude form of trademark protection.

Guilds were extremely important in their day, just as their modern equivalents still are. History professor L. Kip Wheeler points out that,

A fifteenth-century illustration (opposite) depicts seamstresses at work as the tailor sees to a customer in his shop. The early Middle Ages saw the beginnings of organized guilds for tailors, woodworkers, bakers, and other people with crafts and trades.

with all of the benefits guilds provided, they combined "the qualities of a modern union, a vocational school, a trading corporation, and a product regulations committee."[51]

Besides their useful and practical applications, guilds also served as clubs that bonded their members together socially. A guild might sponsor processions and feasts on religious holidays, for instance, or hold festivals in honor of its patron saint. Patron saints were holy figures to whom guilds looked for protection; for example, Saint Augustine was the patron saint of brewers, while jewelers came under the protection of Saint Eligius.

By the late 800s some hubs of commerce and trade had especially active guilds, such as cities in southern Italy, the Rhine Valley (in what is now Germany), and the Low Countries (today's Netherlands, Belgium, and Luxembourg). Larger cities, such as Paris and London, even established specific neighborhoods for given professions during this period. London's Bread Street is a modern-day relic of this geographic specialization, named for what its craftspeople produced. Occupations eventually became so specialized that, for instance, the guilds for woodcutters in some cities were quite separate from those for wood stackers. Woodcutters found stacking their own wood, rather than hiring a specialist, could be fined.

The Legacy of Writing and Books

In addition to the advent of business-oriented organizations such as guilds and communes, the early Middle Ages also left to later centuries strong legacies in scientific, artistic, and intellectual innovation. Many of these stemmed from the Carolingian Renaissance. One such example was Carolingian minuscule, the improved script introduced under

Charlemagne's direction. It made writing dramatically easier for people to read and understand. Prior to its development, the writing style in Europe was based on Roman or Greek alphabets and was relatively simple. Documents were written in capital letters only, for instance, and were copied in one continuous, unbroken stream with no spaces between words.

These characteristics changed completely with the introduction of Carolingian miniscule. It introduced lowercase letters, spaces between words, and a streamlined, uniform style of forming letters. Carolingian miniscule became the basis for written documents for centuries to come and remains the root of the West's modern written alphabet.

The introduction of Carolingian miniscule did not just make reading and writing easier. It also produced far more wide-ranging, long-term repercussions. For example, it helped standardize communication between parts of the empire by making messages more easily understood.

Books and Music

Connected to Carolingian miniscule, and the wider topic of literacy, was another legacy left by the early Middle Ages: the creation of hand-copied books. This work produced the earliest examples of one of the greatest glories of the entire Middle Ages: illuminated manuscripts.

Illuminated manuscripts were volumes of lavish, colored illustrations and elaborate calligraphy (handwriting), with texts taken from the Bible and other religious writings. They were very beautiful; however, since they were for strictly religious purposes, none of these manuscripts was created simply as an example of visual art. Instead, each served a practical purpose: to continue the all-important work of disseminating religious knowledge and passing it from one generation to the next.

The use of art for religious training can be seen in many other remnants of the early medieval period. Examples include surviving manuscripts, metalwork, carved ivory, mosaics, and other visual art, all of which display technical advances and increasingly wider ranges of artistic styles—but are still religious in nature.

Music, a particular interest of Charlemagne, also benefited from advancements during this time, as clergy within the Frankish realm created increasingly sophisticated forms of church music. In particular, evidence indicates that the first instances of written musical notation— the ancestor of the modern way of writing music—began during this period.

As in all aspects of art, musical notation was used for purposes of worship; in this case, to teach and preserve melodies and words used in the chanted prayers sung by monks. This was just another example of the era's virtual ban on creative works that were not overtly religious. J.M. Roberts comments, "The concept of 'art for art's sake' could never have made less sense than in the early Middle Ages."[52]

The Legacy of Learning

The rise in literacy that came during Charlemagne's rule as a result of his various innovations and the prevalence of illuminated manuscripts led to still another legacy of the era: a significant, lasting contribution to the educational process. In general the degree of education was still very limited; most people in the lower classes, and many in the aristocracy as well, remained illiterate and poorly educated. However, the era's monastic schools established a tradition of educational standards that had dramatic and far-reaching results in later centuries.

A legacy that is equally important in the realm of education concerns the concept of higher education. The great seats of learning that are today known as universities had their roots in the early Middle Ages. They grew out of the groups of scholars that some leaders—most famously Charlemagne—established at their courts. These scholars, for the first time during the medieval period, began to study topics such as medicine, astronomy, chemistry, and philosophy for their own sakes rather than for religious purposes. These learned men (and they were virtually all men) did not by any means drop the religious aspects of their studies; a devout commitment to religion remained a cornerstone of life. But they began to look at the world in other ways as well.

Despite initial resistance, these assemblies of scholars quickly attracted eager students. These groups of teachers and students formed the basis of the first recognizable universities—that is, independent, self-governing schools devoted to teaching, study, debate, and research on a variety of religious and secular matters.

The First Universities

Historians generally agree that the first recognizable universities were established in the Byzantine Empire and the Islamic world in the mid-900s. The earliest Western European institutions—and the first schools to use the Latin term *universitas* to describe themselves—soon followed in Bologna, Italy, and Paris, France. Others, such as Cambridge and Oxford in England, followed.

The radical point of view being explored in universities—that of not seeing subjects through only the lens of strict religion—was slow to gain widespread acceptance. When it did, however, it inspired the great surge of exploration and discovery that took place in the late Middle Ages and Renaissance. Among these were the European explorations to the Americas, Africa, and Asia, as well as such scientific and artistic advances as the printing press and the work of Leonardo da Vinci. In fact, the spirit of inquiry that universities represent—and that began in the early Middle Ages—can still be seen today. Walter Ruegg, a scholar of medieval history, points out that the university is "the only European institution which has preserved its fundamental patterns and its basic social role and functions over the course of history."[53]

The Legacy of Economic and Legal Reforms

The first half of the Middle Ages also left Europe with a legacy of improved economics. Some of the concepts adopted during this period

Improvements in Agriculture

Agriculture was a keystone of the feudal system, and improvements in technology throughout the early Middle Ages vastly improved the growing of crops and thus bolstered feudalism. These, in turn, were the forerunners of still more and better agricultural tools and techniques to come.

One major innovation adopted during this period was an improved plow, much heavier but easier to use than the older style. This better plow, which was in use all over Europe by the ninth century, let farmers prepare ground and sow seed more easily and quickly. Other improvements in tools included the use of scythes, which were much more efficient than sickles; horseshoes and harnesses, which improved the strength and control of horses; and improved wagon-building techniques.

Another dramatically improved practice was the revival of Roman-style two- or three-field planting, in which fields were divided with one left fallow (uncultivated) for a season, keeping the soil in better condition. It has been estimated that this led to a 50 percent rise in farm productivity across northern Europe between the sixth and ninth centuries. Furthermore, influenced by Islamic immigrants, farmers in Spain and Italy used intensive irrigation to improve their crop yield.

had existed since ancient times and would reach still greater sophistication later, but important advances were nonetheless made during this period.

The most significant of these were Charlemagne's economic reforms. Among them was the use of standardized money. Earlier, small kingdoms used a hodgepodge of different kinds of money, coinage that was useless outside of that country's borders. Charlemagne's reforms allowed people all over his kingdom to buy and sell goods easily. Such reforms made commerce much easier and are even today standard practice; one example is the widespread use of the euro as a common currency across Europe.

In addition to economic reforms, the first centuries of the medieval era gave birth to an important development in legal reform. This was the Justinian Code, created in the sixth century by a group of scholars under the supervision of the Eastern Roman emperor for whom it is named. Based on a revision of ancient Roman law, the code simplified and clarified the many conflicting laws governing Justinian's domain. This work became the basis for civil law codes that still exist today in many countries. Indeed, it was of such importance that Edward Gibbon, the great chronicler of the fall of the Roman Empire, asserted, "The richest legacy ever left by one civilization to another was the Justinian Code."[54]

Islamic Advances

Innovations were also arriving during the early centuries of the Middle Ages from outside Europe. Specifically, major scientific, technological, and intellectual breakthroughs were being brought into the border regions of the Eastern Roman Empire and Western Europe from the Islamic world as Muslim invaders and settlers made inroads there.

These Muslims introduced a number of crucial innovations, including the replacement of Roman numerals (that is, I, II, III, and so on) with the much more efficient Arabic system (1, 2, 3, etc.). Muslim scholars also introduced the concept of algebra, the manufacture of complex astronomical instruments, and new and highly developed forms of architecture. Furthermore, Muslim settlers brought with them a great number of agricultural innovations. For instance, immigrants to Sicily and other areas of the Mediterranean introduced efficient methods of crop production and brought such plants as lemons, oranges, and mulberries with them.

Invaluable Legacies

Clearly, the early Middle Ages created a number of invaluable legacies, both to the following era—the late Middle Ages—and to the centuries beyond. Innovations in virtually every aspect of life, from the structure of societies and governments to methods of planting crops and writing documents, started during this time. It is true that there were negative aspects of the early Middle Ages; the era's record of violence, oppression, and ignorance cannot be denied. Nonetheless, and contrary to the popular image of the "Dark Ages," the early Middle Ages created an important series of precedents for civilizations yet to come.

Source Notes

Introduction: The Defining Characteristics of the Early Middle Ages

1. Quoted in "Every Genealogists' Dream Descent: From Charlemagne, King of Franks, Emperor of Holy Roman Empire," History KB.com, January 2009. www.historykb.com.
2. J.M. Roberts, *A History of Europe*. New York: Allen Lane/Penguin, 1996, p. 79.
3. Colin McEvedy, *The New Penguin Atlas of Medieval History*. New York: Penguin, 1992, p. 8.
4. Peter S. Wells, *Barbarians to Angels: The Dark Ages Reconsidered*. New York: Norton, 2008, p. 200.

Chapter One: What Events Led to the Early Middle Ages?

5. Quoted in Wells, *Barbarians to Angels*, p. xii.
6. McEvedy, *The New Penguin Atlas of Medieval History*, p. 8.
7. Roberts, *A History of Europe*, p. 70.
8. Quoted in Susan Wise Bauer, *The History of the Medieval World: From the Conversion of Constantine to the First Crusade*. New York: Norton, 2010, p. 432.
9. Quoted in Bauer, *The History of the Medieval World*, p. 467.
10. Quoted in Bauer, *The History of the Medieval World*, p. 109.
11. Quoted in Bauer, *The History of the Medieval World*, p. 262.
12. Quoted in Wells, *Barbarians to Angels*, p. 7.
13. Chris Wickham, *The Inheritance of Rome: Illuminating the Dark Ages, 400–1000*. New York: Viking, 2009, p. 107.
14. Edward Gibbon, *The History of the Decline and Fall of the Roman Empir*, 1776. www.his.com.
15. Roberts, *A History of Europe*, p. 60.

16. Wells, *Barbarians to Angels*, p. 4.

17. McEvedy, *The New Penguin Atlas of Medieval History*, p. 32.

18. Roberts, *A History of Europe*, p. 110.

Chapter Two: The Rise of Kingdoms

19. Geoffrey Barraclough, *The Crucible of Europe: The Ninth and Tenth Centuries in European History*. Berkeley: University of California Press, 1976, p. 13.

20. McEvedy, *The New Penguin Atlas of Medieval History*, p. 44.

21. Quoted in "Every Genealogists' Dream Descent."

22. Barraclough, *The Crucible of Europe*, p. 54.

23. Roberts, *A History of Europe*, pp. 83–84.

24. Wickham, *The Inheritance of Rome*, p. 259.

Chapter Three: The Power of the Church

25. Wickham, *The Inheritance of Rome*, p. 52.

26. Roberts, *A History of Europe*, p. 106.

27. McEvedy, *The New Penguin Atlas of Medieval History*, p. 22.

28. Quoted in Bauer, *The History of the Medieval World*, p. 173.

29. McEvedy, *The New Penguin Atlas of Medieval History*, p. 54.

30. Quoted in Bauer, *The History of the Medieval World*, p. 148.

31. Roberts, *A History of Europe*, p. 110.

32. "Einhard: The Life of Charlemagne," trans. Samuel Epes Turner, 1880, Internet Medieval Sourcebook, January 1999. www.fordham.edu.

33. Barraclough, *The Crucible of Europe*, p. 45.

34. Quoted in Bauer, *The History of the Medieval World*, p. 394.

35. Henri Pirenne, *Mohammed and Charlemagne*. Mineola, NY: Dover, 2001, p. 234.

36. McEvedy, *The New Penguin Atlas of Medieval History*, p. 72.

Chapter Four: The Rise of Feudalism

37. Marjorie Rowling, *Everyday Life in Medieval Times*. New York: Dorset, 1968, p. 124.

38. Kenneth Jupp, "European Feudalism from Its Emergence Through Its Decline," *American Journal of Economics and Sociology*, December 2000. http://findarticles.com.

39. Quoted in Peter Speed, ed., *Those Who Fought: An Anthology of Medieval Sources*. New York: Italica, 1996, p. 95.

40. Roberts, *A History of Europe*, p. 132.

41. Wickham, *The Inheritance of Rome*, p. 191.

42. Roberts, *A History of Europe*, p. 132.

43. Jupp, "European Feudalism from Its Emergence Through Its Decline."

44. Wells, *Barbarians to Angels*, p. 101.

45. Quoted in "Climate Changes of 535 to 536," Science Daily, 2010. www.sciencedaily.com.

Chapter Five: What Is the Legacy of the Early Middle Ages?

46. Richard Hooker, "The French," European Middle Ages, 1996. http://wsu.edu.

47. Gianfranco Poggi, *The Development of the Modern State*. Palo Alto, CA: Stanford University Press, 1978, p. 32.

48. Quoted in Poggi, *The Development of the Modern State*, p. 33.

49. E.L. Knox, "Medieval Society," History of Western Civilization, 2010. www.boisestate.edu.

50. William W. Kibler, ed., *Medieval France: An Encyclopedia*. Oxford: Routledge, 1995, p. 245.

51. L. Kip Wheeler, "Guilds," *Medieval Studies*, September 30, 2010. http://web.cn.edu.

52. Roberts, *A History of Europe*, p. 124.

53. Quoted in Hilde de Ridder-Symoens, ed., *A History of the University in Europe*. Vol. 1, *Universities in the Middle Ages*. Cambridge: Cambridge University Press, 2003, p. ii.

54. Quoted in Rossiter Johnson, ed., *The Great Events by Famous Historians*. Whitefish, MT: Kessinger, 2004, p. 138.

Important People of the Early Middle Ages

Charlemagne: King of the Franks from 771 to 814 and emperor of the Romans from 800 to 814; the most influential individual of the era, he formed the first large European empire since the Romans and was instrumental in spreading Christianity and bringing about important social, economic, and artistic reforms.

Charles Martel: Charlemagne's grandfather and the ruler for whom the Carolingian dynasty in the Frankish Empire is named.

Clovis: The first king to unite all of the Frankish tribes; he founded the Merovingian dynasty in the Frankish Empire that Charlemagne greatly expanded.

Constantine: The first Christian Roman emperor; he also presided over the establishment of Constantinople (today, Istanbul) as the center of the Eastern Roman Empire.

Pope Gregory I: Gregory the Great, as he is known, created important reforms in church practices, notably in how religious rituals were carried out; he also greatly expanded the practice of missionary work to spread Christianity.

Justinian I: One of the most notable rulers of the Byzantine Empire; enacted important legal reforms.

Leo III: A close ally of Charlemagne and the pope who crowned him emperor of the Romans.

Odoacer: The first emperor of the Roman Empire to come from outside the empire; he assumed power in 456 after the collapse of the Western Empire.

Otto the Great: The first ruler, named in 962, of what became the Holy Roman Empire.

For Further Research

Books

Mike Corbishley, *The Middle Ages.* New York: Chelsea House, 2007.

Madeleine Pelner Cosman and Linda Gale Jones, *Handbook to Life in the Medieval World.* New York: Facts On File, 2008.

John Davenport, *The Age of Feudalism.* Farmington Hills, MI: Lucent, 2007.

Ruth Tenzer Feldman, *The Fall of Constantinople.* Minneapolis: Twenty-First Century, 2008.

Norman Bancroft Hunt, *Living in the Middle Ages.* New York: Chelsea House, 2008.

Rita J. Markel, *The Fall of the Roman Empire.* Minneapolis: Twenty-First Century, 2008.

Don Nardo, *Lords, Ladies, Peasants, and Knights: Class in the Middle Ages.* Farmington Hills, MI: Lucent, 2007.

John Thompson, *The Medieval World: An Illustrated Atlas.* Washington, DC: National Geographic, 2010.

Chris Wickham, *Framing the Early Middle Ages: Europe and the Mediterranean, 400–800.* New York: Oxford University Press, 2007.

———, *The Inheritance of Rome: Illuminating the Dark Ages, 400–1000.* New York: Viking, 2009.

Websites

"Dark Ages History," History Times.com (www.historytimes.com/fresh-perspectives-in-history/dark-ages-history). Maintained by British history specialists, this site offers a large number of articles on specific topics about early medieval times. It is not written for students and is too specialized for general research, but it is very useful for finding information on a particular subject.

Enter the Middle Ages (www.mnsu.edu/emuseum/history/middle ages). This cleverly designed site is maintained by Minnesota State University. It lets visitors choose a figure (knight, nun, etc.) to "guide" them through different aspects of medieval life.

Full-Text Resources for "Dark Age" History (www.kmatthews.org.uk/history/texts.html). A portal for sites providing complete texts of primary source material from the fifth to the seventh century in England.

Internet Medieval Sourcebook (www.fordham.edu/halsall/sbook.html). A huge site maintained by a faculty member at Fordham University that includes texts from a variety of primary sources.

The Middle Ages.net (www.themiddleages.net). This site has a lot of clearly written and detailed information about the medieval era, such as music, feudalism, weapons, and daily life.

Virtual Library Medieval Europe Index (www.msu.edu/%7Egeor gem1/history/medieval.htm). A portal leading to a wide variety of sites on specific topics, maintained by the History Department of Michigan State University. Through it, researchers can find sites on particular areas, such as medieval weapons or food production.

Index

Picture Credits

About the Author

Adam Woog has written many books for adults, young adults, and children. He has a special interest in history. Woog lives with his wife in Seattle, Washington, and they have a daughter in college.